# MILE-A-MINUTE
## QUILTS

### Sharon Hultgren

Produced for Leisure Arts by The Creative Partners™ LLC

Linda Causee, Editor

Carol Wilson Mansfield, Photo Stylist

Ann Harnden, Copy Editor

Wayne Norton, Photography

Graphic Solutions inc-chgo, Book Design

Produced by The Creative Partners™

# ACKNOWLEDGMENTS

I would like to thank first of all my husband, Dale, who understood when I disappeared down to my studio and only came up for food and sleep. Don't picture me in a dark, dank basement! I have wonderful, big windows that look out toward the lake. There is a door nearby that I escape out of to catch a breath of fresh air and enjoy the quiet of the woods and water.

I would like to thank my mom and dad who have been understanding when my visits have not been as frequent as both of us would of liked. They would call and remind me to keep working!

Thanks to my children and grandchildren who understand when the cookie jar is not full and grandma is "still working" on the book.

To Gayle Camargo, my friend and encourager: thanks for the boxes of fabric that are seen in the quilts in this book. Thanks also to my friends at Benartex, Inc.

Thanks to those who helped me stitch the seam covers: daughter, Pam Klein; daughter-in-law, Karla Hultgren; granddaughters, Stephanie Klein and Madison Hultgren; grandson, Jackson Hultgren; and friend, Patty Goodman; (grandsons, Zach Klein and Tyler Hultgren were interested in what I was doing, but not ready to pick up a needle and thread!)

A big thank you to Rene Aden who did most of the quilting in this book. As fast as I was designing and piecing, she was quilting for me. I am glad it didn't get too cold before the book was finished, and she was able to keep Jim here in the north country until we were done!

A special thanks to EZ Quilting by Wrights for bringing to market the special tools that Darlene Zimmerman and I designed to help quilters. These tools made my Mile-A-Miute quilts go even faster.

And, thank you to Rita Weiss of Creative Partners, who challenged me to write this book and Linda Causee who made my quilt directions look good and my book pretty.

I am blessed and thankful.

*Sharon*

# INTRODUCTION

"Now you are ready to quilt your quilt!"

These words are wonderful to hear because they mean you have finished piecing the top of your quilt or wall hanging. But! They also mean your quilt is not complete and ready for use until the actual quilting process is done. This brings up the question, "How do you plan to finish your quilt?" Unfortunately, many quilt tops end up in a drawer for the next generation to finish or to become part of an estate sale.

Long ago most quilts were quilted by hand. Some were done as a social in a church basement or in a large hoop in the living room. Many quilters tell stories of the women in their family quilting around a large frame that consumed a spare room.

In the mid 1980's we began to see beautiful quilting being done by sewing machine. Harriet Hargrave was one of the pioneers of this process. Then Debra Wagner began to win "best of show" awards at national quilting shows with her exquisite machine quilting, and real interest was born in finishing your quilt in the same way it was started, by machine. Today machine quilting is an industry all its own with commercial machines and people who earn their living by quilting tops for their piecing friends and customers.

Often the home sewer who has pieced a top would love to finish her quilt by machine, but this can be a cumbersome task. First, there is finding a large enough area to lay out and secure the backing fabric. Then the batting must be carefully positioned on top of the backing, making sure there are no wrinkles or bulges. Then, the pieced top is stretched on top of these layers. Next, the layers must be secured by hand stitching large basting stitches or safety pins. If there is a quilting design, the marking must be done before the stitching begins.

At last, the quilt is ready and taken to the machine, This is no small task. Great care must be taken so that the quilt does not bunch up, so that sewing needles are not broken, and the quilter is not burdened down with the immenseness of the big quilt.

I have experienced all of these problems as I tried to machine quilt my quilts. I kept thinking, there must be a better way!

Mile-a-Minute quilting was the answer for me! Now I can plan any size quilt I need, and finish it on panels that are 20" wide. At first I started by cutting the panels myself before I began my quilting project. This was a somewhat cumbersome procedure. Why couldn't batting come in 20" widths? So, I invented Roll and Quilt™ which is produced today by Airtex® and is available at your local quilt shop. This is not a new concept, but it is a new product. We don't have to cut our own batting. It is ready for us with no wrinkles or stretched-out areas.

The patterns in this book were designed for this process. You can, of course, cut your own panels, but using Roll and Quilt™ will make your quilting move along at just about a mile a minute.

Once you have completed all of the panels, the question becomes, "How do you sew the panels together?" I wanted this to be as easy as possible. I found that after the quilting is completed and the panel is carefully trimmed to the edges of the pieced top, the seams are just sewn together, all layers included. Then, the seam is pressed open, and a folded piece of fabric—I call a seam cover—is placed over the seam and hand or machine sewn on. The seams can be brought to the front and the seam cover becomes part of the design. It's simple; it's quick.

I hope you enjoy the Mile-a-Minute process and are able to complete your own quilts on your own sewing machine.

# TABLE OF CONTENTS

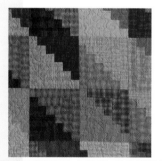
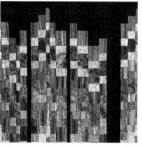

**NATURE STUDIES NINE PATCH**
63

**ALL STAR SALUTE**
97

**HERE'S MY HEART**
70

**STARS BY DESIGN**
103

**WINTER PINES**
79

**WINDFLOWER**
111

**HAPPY BIRTHDAY**
91

**CUBES IN A ROW**
118

# GENERAL DIRECTIONS

### JUST WHAT ARE MILE-A-MINUTE QUILTS?

Mile-a-Minute Quilts are quilts that are made up of individually quilted panels. The panel is a narrow part of the whole quilt. The pieced panels in this book are 20" wide for the most part. The panel can be any length and there can be as many panels as the quilt requires. After the panel is pieced it is layered with a batting and backing. Then it is either basted or pinned with safety pins. The panel is then quilted. A narrow panel is much easier for the home quilter to maneuver through a sewing machine than a large quilt that is hanging all over the quilter.

### HOW TO MAKE A MILE-A-MINUTE QUILT

The instructions for making the panels for your quilt are given with the individual quilt instructions.

For several of the quilts I give you alternate instructions using tools from EZ Quilting by Wrights including the Companion Angle™, Easy Hexagon™, Easy Eight™, Easy Six™, and Easy Three™. These tools can be purchased at your local quilt shop or department. While you can make the quilts without these tools, they will help to make your work even faster. I have not given you basic quilt making instructions because I am assuming that you know how to make quilts. You just want to make them faster!

### LAYERING AND QUILTING

Cut the batting and backing panels so they are 1" to 2" larger than the pieced panel along along all sides.

*Note: If the pieced panel is wider than the 20" width of the batting, you will have to piece two pieces of batting. Place batting pieces next to each other and hand stitch together using cross stitches.* **(Diagram 1)**

Diagram 1

Place backing on a flat surface with wrong side up. Smooth out batting on top. Center the pieced panel on batting. Baste the layers together by hand or with safety pins.

Quilt as desired using a walking foot to feed the layers of the quilt panels evenly through the machine.

**Quilting in the Ditch** is one of the easiest ways to machine quilt. Using your fingers, pull the blocks or pieces apart slightly and machine stitch right between the two pieces. The stitching will look better if you keep the stitching to the side of the seam that does not have the extra bulk of the seam allowance under it. The quilting will be hidden in the seam.

**Free-form Machine Quilting** can be used to quilt around a design or to quilt a motif. The quilting is done with a darning foot and the feed dogs down on the sewing machine. It takes practice to master free-form quilting because you are controlling the movement of the quilt under the needle rather than the sewing machine moving the quilt. You can quilt in any direction—up and down, side-to-side and even in circles—without pivoting the quilt around the needle. Practice this quilting method before trying it on your quilt.

When the quilting on the panel is complete, press panel lightly from the back side. Trim the edges even with the pieced panels except where the outside edges of the quilt will be covered with binding. At the outer edges, allow a little extra batting so that the binding will be full.

## COVERING THE SEAMS

After pressing and trimming, join the panels with a quarter inch seam allowance. It is important to match the piecing in the blocks with the joining panels. The seams can be on top or on the back. If it is on the top, the seam covers will be part of the design of the quilt such as in *Basket Weave*, page 13, *Front Porch Swing*, page 18, and *All Star Salute*, page 97. If they are on the backing side, the seam covers will become part of the backing as in the remaining quilts.

To cover the seams, first measure the length of the quilted panels. Piece and cut $2^1/2$"-wide strips to that measurement.

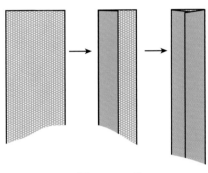

Fold the strip in thirds with wrong sides together. **(Diagram 2)**

Place folded strip with raw edge down on top of seam. Hand or machine stitch along both folded edges. **(Diagram 3)** Repeat for all seams.

Diagram 2

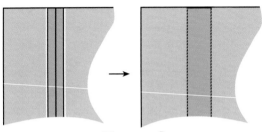

Diagram 3

## ADDING CONTINUOUS BINDING

Once the quilt has been quilted, the edges must be bound. Start by trimming the backing and batting even with the quilt top. Measure the quilt top and cut enough 2¹/₂" wide strips to go around all four sides of the quilt plus 12". Join the strips end to end with diagonal seams and trim the corners. Press the seams open. **(Diagram 4)**

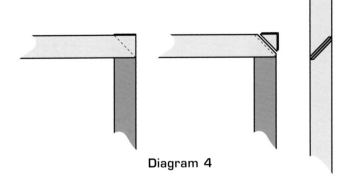

Diagram 4

Cut one end of the strip at a 45-degree angle and press under ¹/₄". Press entire strip in half lengthwise, wrong sides together. **(Diagram 5)**

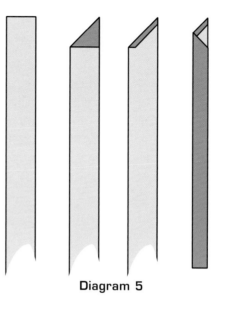

**Diagram 5**

On the back of the quilt, position the binding in the middle of one side, keeping the raw edges together. Sew the binding to the quilt with the ¹/₄" seam allowance, beginning about three inches below the folded end of the binding. **(Diagram 6)**

At the corner, stop ¹/₄" from the edge of the quilt and backstitch.

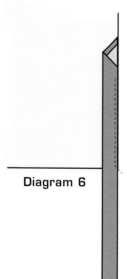

**Diagram 6**

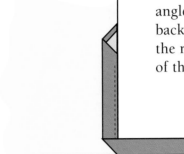

Fold binding away from quilt so it is at a right angle to edge just sewn. Then, fold the binding back on itself so the fold is on the quilt edge and the raw edges are aligned with the adjacent side of the quilt. **(Diagram 7)**

Begin sewing at the quilt edge. **(Diagram 8)** Continue in the same way around the remaining sides of the quilt. Stop about 2" away from the starting point. Trim any excess binding and tuck it inside the folded end. Finish the stitching.

**Diagram 7**

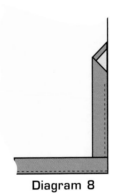

**Diagram 8**

Fold the binding to the front of the quilt so the seam line is covered; machine-stitch the binding in place on the front of the quilt. Use a straight stitch or tiny zigzag with invisible or matching thread. If you have a sewing machine that does embroidery stitches, you may want to use your favorite stitch. **(Diagram 9)**

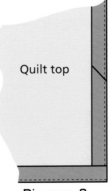

Quilt top

**Diagram 9**

# BASKET WEAVE

Approximate Size: 58" x 70"

## MATERIALS

   8 assorted fat quarters, pink

   8 assorted fat quarters, green

   2 yards dark print (seam covers/sashing, border, binding)

   4 yards backing

   1 package Roll and Quilt™ batting

## CUTTING

### Blocks

   14 strips, 2$\frac{1}{2}$" x 8$\frac{1}{2}$" each, pink and green

### Finishing

   4 strips, 2$\frac{1}{2}$"-wide, dark print, seam covers

   6 strips, 3$\frac{1}{2}$" x 16$\frac{1}{2}$", dark print, top and bottom borders

   4 strips, 3$\frac{1}{2}$"-wide, dark print, side borders

   7 strips, 2$\frac{1}{2}$"-wide, dark print, binding

   3 panels, 20" x 72", backing fabric

14

## INSTRUCTIONS

### Blocks

1. Sew four different green strips together. **(Diagram 1)** Make a total of 24 green blocks.

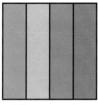

Diagram 1

2. Sew four different pink strips together. **(Diagram 2)** Make a total of 24 pink blocks.

Diagram 2

3. Sew green and pink blocks together in pairs. **(Diagram 3)**

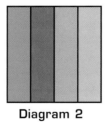

Diagram 3

### Finishing

1. Sew eight pairs of blocks to form a panel. **(Diagram 4)** Repeat for two more panels.

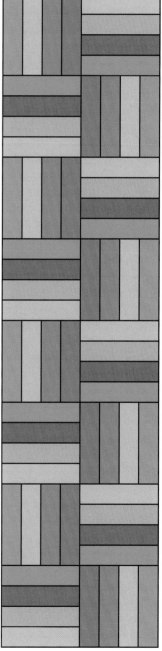

Diagram 4

2. Sew a 3½" x 16½" dark print strip to the top and bottom of each panel. **(Diagram 5)**

**Diagram 5**

3. For side borders, sew 3½" strips together to make a 70½" strip; repeat.

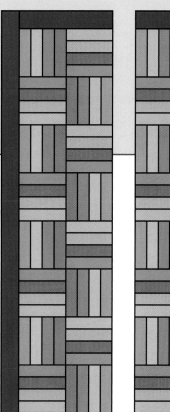
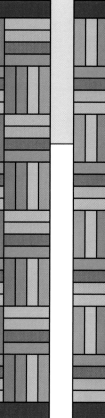
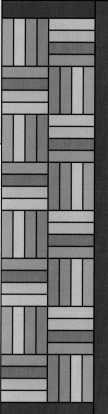

4. Sew a border strip to the left side of one (first) panel and right side of another (third) panel. **(Diagram 6)**

5. Layer each panel with batting and backing. Quilt as desired.

6. Sew panels together with **backing** sides together.  Hide seams referring to Covering the Seams, page 9. Note that seam covers will be the sashing between panels.

7. Bind quilt referring to Adding Continuous Binding, page 10.

Diagram 6

**Basket Weave Layout**

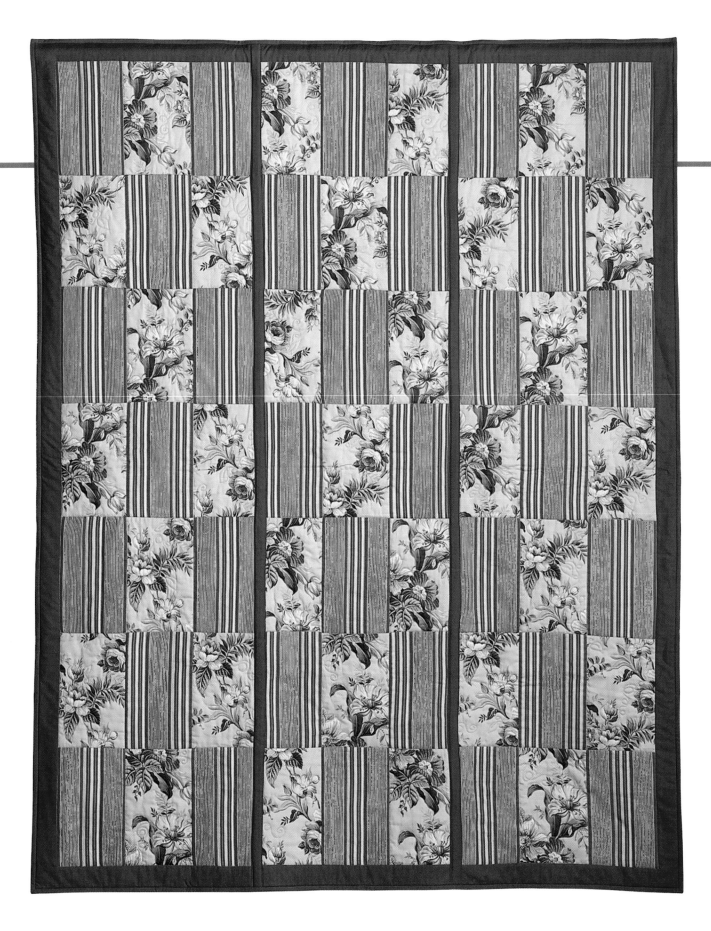

# FRONT PORCH SWING

Approximate Size: 58" x 74"

## MATERIALS

- 2 yards floral print
- 2 yards stripe
- 1 1/2 yards dark solid (border, binding)
- 4 1/2 yards backing
- 1 package Roll and Quilt™ batting

## CUTTING

### Blocks

6 floral print strips, 10 1/2"-wide
cut into 32 rectangles, 6 1/2" x 10 1/2"

6 stripe strips, 10 1/2"-wide
cut into 32 rectangles, 6 1/2" x 10 1/2"

### Finishing

6 dark solid strips, 2 1/2" x 18 1/2"
(top/bottom borders)

8 dark solid strips, 2 1/2"-wide (side
borders, seam covers/sashing)

7 dark solid strips, 2 1/2"-wide (binding)

3 panels, 20" x 76", backing fabric

# FRONT PORCH SWING

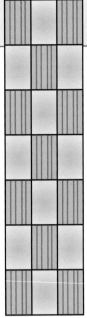

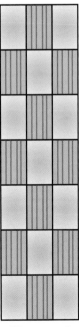

Diagram 1

## INSTRUCTIONS

### Blocks

1. For the first and third panels, sew rectangles in seven rows of three alternating stripe and floral prints. **(Diagram 1)**

2. For the second panel, sew rectangles in seven rows of three alternating floral and stripe prints. **(Diagram 2)**

3. Sew a $2\frac{1}{2}$" x $18\frac{1}{2}$" dark solid strip to top and bottom of each panel. **(Diagram 3)**

Diagram 2

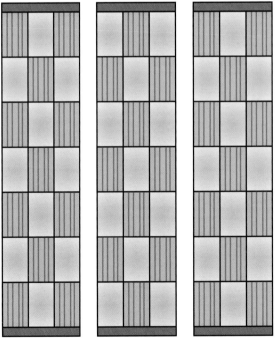

Diagram 3

### Finishing

1. Piece 2 1/2"-wide dark solid strips 74 1/2" long; repeat.  Sew one strip to the left side of panel one and the right side of panel three. **(Diagram 4)**

2. Layer backing, batting and panels. Quilt as desired.

3. Sew panels together with **backing** sides together. *Note: Seam will be on front side of quilt.* Hide seams referring to Covering the Seams, page 9. Note that the seam covers become the sashing between panels on front of the quilt.

4. Add binding referring to Adding Continuous Binding, page 10.

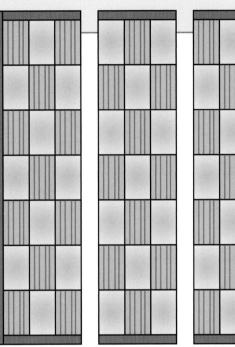

Diagram 4

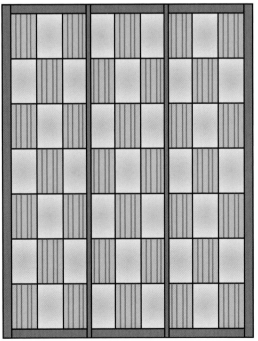

**Front Porch Swing Layout**

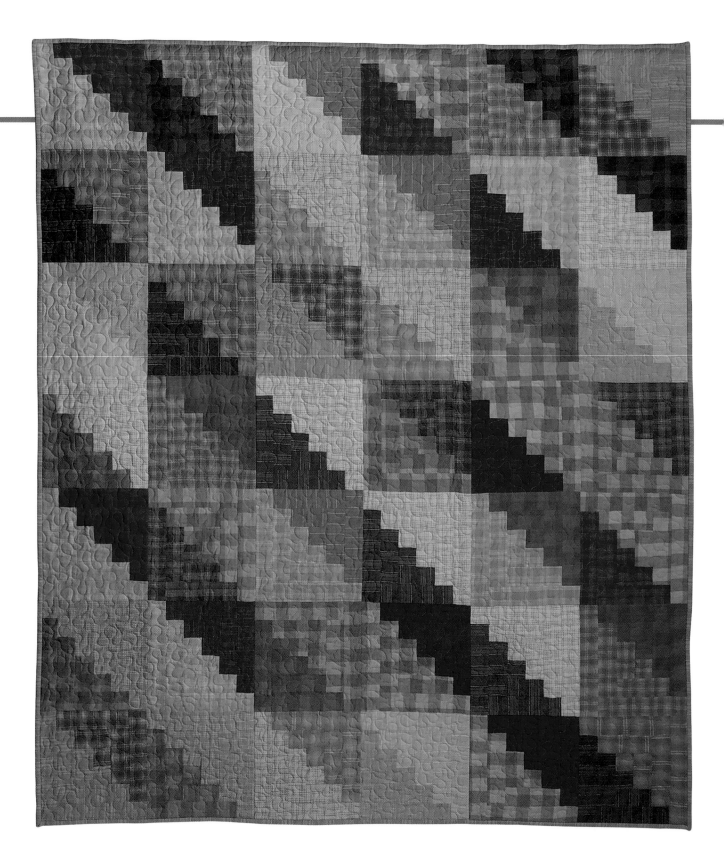

# FIRESIDE LOG CABIN

Approximate Size: 54" x 63"

## MATERIALS

2 yards assorted dark fabrics

2¹/₂ yards assorted light fabrics

1 yard binding (includes seam covers)

4 yards backing

1 package Roll and Quilt™ batting

## CUTTING

**Blocks**

Cut all light and dark fabrics into 2"-wide strips. Then cut 42 of each of the following:

2" x 2" squares, dark fabric (center square)

2" x 2" squares, light fabric (Log 2)

2" x 3¹/₂" strips, light fabric (Log 3)

2" x 3¹/₂" strips, dark fabric (Log 4)

2" x 5" strips, dark fabric (Log 5)

2" x 5" strips, light fabric (Log 6)

2" x 6¹/₂" strips, light fabric (Log 7)

2" x 6¹/₂" strips, dark fabric (Log 8)

2" x 8" strips, dark fabric (Log 9)

2" x 8" strips, light fabric (Log 10)

2" x 9¹/₂" strips, light fabric (Log 11)

*cutting directions continue on page 24*

# FIRESIDE LOG CABIN

Diagram 1

### Finishing

11 strips, 2$^1$/$_2$"-wide (seam covers, binding)

3 panels, 20" x 65", backing fabric (backing)

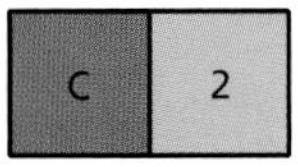

## INSTRUCTIONS

### Blocks

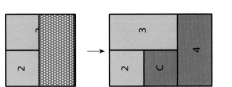

Diagram 2

1. Sew a 2" light and a 2" dark square together. **(Diagram 1)** Press seam toward dark square.

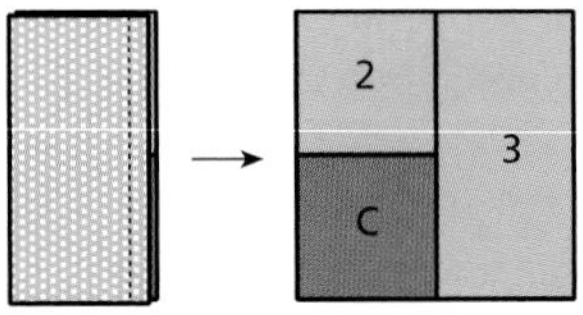

2. Turn unit just made so light square is at top; sew to a 2" x 3$^1$/$_2$" light strip. **(Diagram 2)**

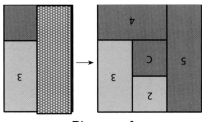

Diagram 3

3. Turn unit so light strip just added is at top; sew to a 2" x 3$^1$/$_2$" dark strip. **(Diagram 3)**

4. Continue turning and adding strips until block is completed. **(Diagrams 4 - 10)** Make a total of 42 Log Cabin blocks.

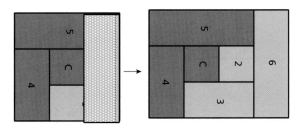

Diagram 4

Diagram 5

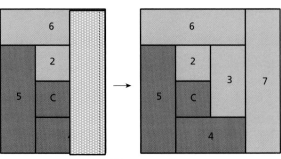

Diagram 6

24

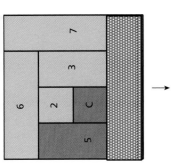
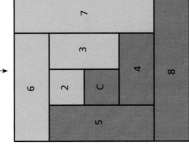
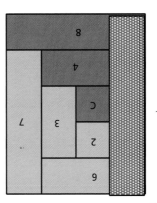
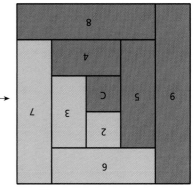

**Diagram 7**

**Diagram 8**

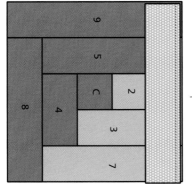

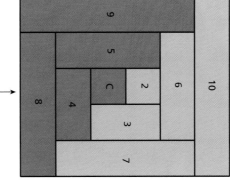

**Diagram 9**

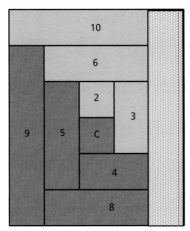

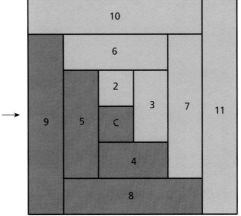

**Diagram 10**

# FIRESIDE LOG CABIN

Diagram 11

**Finishing**

1. Place blocks in seven rows of six referring to layout or your own design.

2. Sew blocks together in pairs. Sew pairs together to form panels. **(Diagram 11)**

3. Layer panels with batting and backing. Quilt as desired.

4. Sew quilted panels with right sides together. Hide seams referring to Covering the Seams, page 9.

5. Add binding referring to Adding Continuous Binding, page 10.

Fireside Log Cabin Layout

# FRIENDSHIP PARADE

Approximate Size: 65" x 72"

## MATERIALS

12 assorted print fat quarters

3 yards white (borders, sashing)

$5/8$ yard binding fabric

$4^{1/2}$ yards backing (includes seam covers)

1 package Quilt and Roll™ batting

Template plastic

## CUTTING

**Quilt Strips**

6 strips each, 3"-wide, assorted print fat quarters

**Finishing**

2 lengthwise strips, $3^{1/2}$"-wide, white (side borders)

6 lengthwise strips, $2^{1/2}$"-wide, white (sashing)

2 strips, $3^{1/2}$" x $15^{1/2}$", white (top/bottom borders)

4 strips, $3^{1/2}$" x $17^{1/2}$", white (top/bottom borders)

2 strips, $3^{1/2}$" x $8^{1/2}$", white, (top/bottom borders)

3 panels, 20" x 75", backing fabric (backing panels)

1 panel, 12" x 75", backing fabric(backing panels)

6 strips, $2^{1/2}$"-wide, backing fabric (seam covers)

8 strips, $2^{1/2}$"-wide, white (binding)

## INSTRUCTIONS

### Strips

1. Place two 3"-wide print strips right sides together. Be sure to line up strips evenly. Measure 6⁷⁄₈" from one short end of strip pair and place acrylic ruler at a 45 degree angle. **(Diagram 1)**

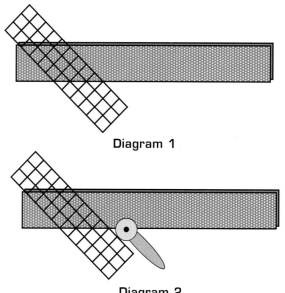

Diagram 1

Diagram 2

2. Cut strip along edge of ruler. **(Diagram 2)** You will have two trapezoids that are mirror images. **(Diagram 3)**

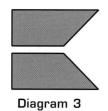

Diagram 3

*Hint: Make a plastic template of the trapezoid just cut to use as a guide for cutting remaining pieces.*

3. Continue cutting strips along entire length of strip pair. **(Diagram 4)**

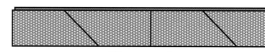

Diagram 4

4. Repeat for remaining pairs of strips.

5. For braided strip, place two mirror image strips right sides together; sew. Press open. **(Diagram 5)**

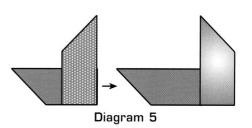

Diagram 5

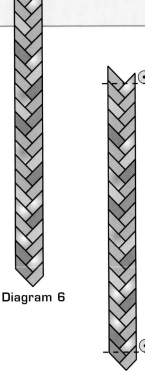

Diagram 6

Diagram 7

6. Continue adding assorted trapezoids until desired length is achieved. Photographed quilt uses 40 print trapezoids for each strip. **(Diagram 6)**

7. Trim excess at top and bottom of each strip. **(Diagram 7)**

8. Make six more strips in same manner.

**Finishing**

1. Make four vertical panels by sewing 2 1/2"-wide white sashing strips to braided strips. **(Diagram 8)**

Diagram 8

2. Sew 3 1/2"-wide strips to top and bottom of each panel. **(Diagram 9)**

3. Sew one 3 1/2"-wide side border strip to left edge of first panel and the other 3 1/2"-wide side border strip to right edge of fourth panel. **(Diagram 10)**

3 1/2" x 15 1/2"    3 1/2" x 17 1/2"    3 1/2" x 17 1/2"    3 1/2" x 8 1/2"

Diagram 9

Diagram 10

**Friendship Parade Layout**

4. Layer panels with batting and backing. Quilt as desired.

5. Sew panels right sides together. Hide seams referring to Covering the Seams, page 9.

6. Bind quilt referring to Adding Continuous Binding, page 10.

## ALTERNATE CUTTING USING EASY ANGLE™ TOOL

Follow instructions above to make quilt except use the Easy Angle™ tool to cut assorted print strips into trapezoids. **(Diagram 1)**

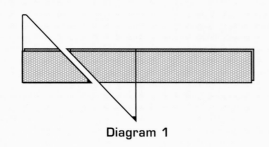

Diagram 1

# DOUBLE DUTCH

Approximate Size: 54" x 70"

## MATERIALS

2 1/2 yards white (blocks, sashing)

3/8 yard each, 6 assorted blue fabrics (blocks)

3/4 yard dark blue (border)

3/4 yard dark blue (binding)

4 yards backing (includes seam covers)

1 package Roll and Quilt™ batting

## CUTTING

### Blocks

2 strips each, 4 3/8"-wide, blue fabrics

12 strips, 4 3/8"-wide, white

### Finishing

13 strips, 2 1/2" x 14 1/2", white (horizontal sashing)

2 strips, 2 1/2" x 18 1/2", white (horizontal sashing)

8 strips, 2 1/2"-wide, white (lengthwise sashing)

4 strips, 2 1/2" x 14 1/2", dark blue (top/bottom border)

2 strips, 2 1/2" x 18 1/2", dark blue (top/bottom border)

4 strips, 2 1/2"-wide, dark blue (side borders)

4 squares, 4 1/2" x 4 1/2", dark blue (cornerstones)

4 strips, 2 1/2"-wide, backing fabric (seam covers)

3 panels, 20" x 72", backing fabric (backing)

7 strips, 2 1/2"-wide, dark blue (binding)

34

## INSTRUCTIONS

### Blocks

1. Place a 4³/₈" blue strip and 4³/₈" white strip right sides together. Cut eight pairs of squares. (**Diagram 1**) Repeat for all blue and

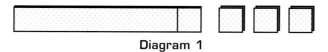

Diagram 1

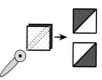

Diagram 2

white strips for a total of 96 pairs of squares.

2. Using a pencil or fabric marking tool, draw a diagonal line on wrong side of white squares. (**Diagram 2**) Be sure to keep pairs of squares together.

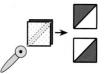

Diagram 3

3. Sew ¹/₄" from each side of drawn line of each pair of blue and white squares. (**Diagram 3**) Cut along drawn line to make two half-square triangles. (**Diagram 4**) You will have 192 half-square triangles.

Diagram 4

4. Sew half-square triangles into pairs using the same blue fabric triangles in each pair. (**Diagram 5**)

Diagram 5

5. Sew pairs of half-square triangles together using the same blue fabric. (**Diagram 6**) You will have 48 Pinwheel blocks.

6. Sew two different Pinwheel blocks together; repeat using the same-color blue Pinwheel blocks. (**Diagram 7**) Block should measure 14¹/₂" x 14¹/₂".

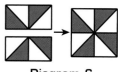

Diagram 6

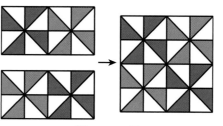

Diagram 7

7. Repeat for 11 more blocks using two different shades of blue in each block.

**Finishing**

1. Sew four blocks alternating with three $2^{1}/_{2}$" x $14^{1}/_{2}$" white sashing strips to make a vertical panel. **(Diagram 8)** Repeat for two more panels.

2. Sew a $2^{1}/_{2}$"-wide white sashing strip to each side of middle panel. **(Diagram 9)**

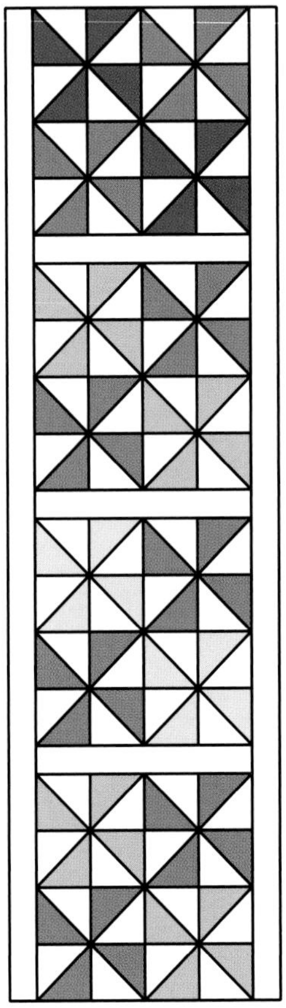

3. Sew a white $2^{1}/_{2}$" x $18^{1}/_{2}$" and a dark blue $2^{1}/_{2}$" x $18^{1}/_{2}$" strip to top and bottom of middle panel. **(Diagram 10)**

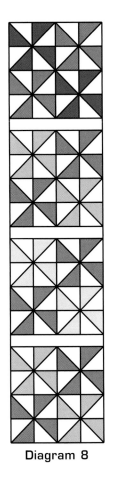

Diagram 8

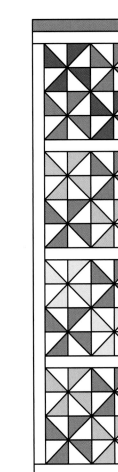

Diagram 9

Diagram 10

4. Sew a white 2$^1$/$_2$" x 14$^1$/$_2$" strip and a dark blue 2$^1$/$_2$" x 14$^1$/$_2$" strip to top and bottom of remaining panels. **(Diagram 11)**

5. For side borders, sew 2$^1$/$_2$"-wide white and dark blue strips together. Sew a 4$^1$/$_2$" dark square to each end. **(Diagram 12)** Repeat.

Diagram 11

Diagram 12

6. Referring to Quilt Layout, page 38, sew border strip to left side of first panel and right side of third panel.

7. Layer each panel with batting and backing. Quilt as desired.

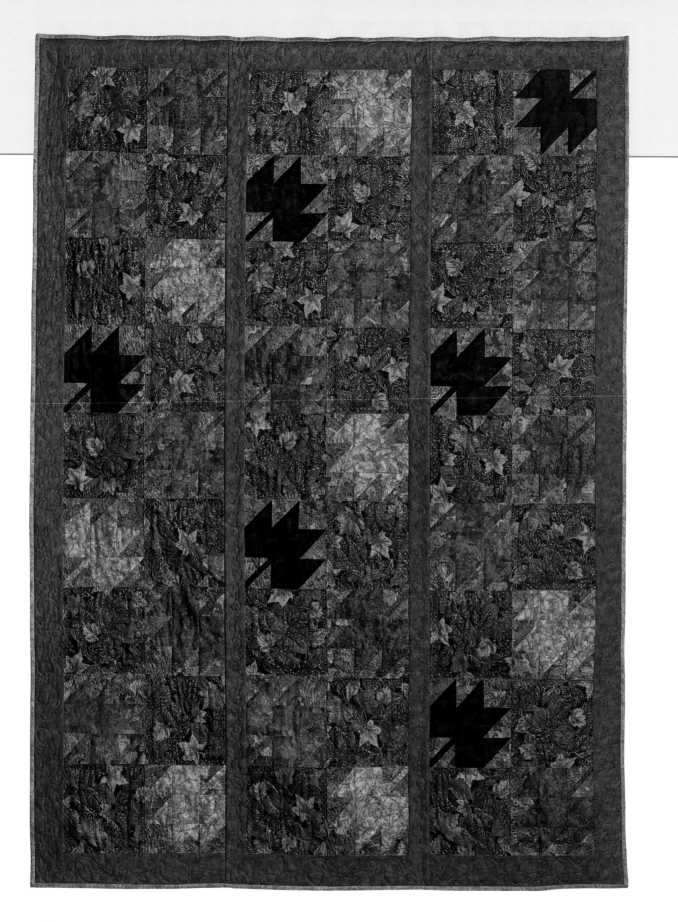

40

**Finishing**

4 strips, 2½"-wide, rust (sashing)

6 strips, 3½" x 15½" strips, rust (border)

4 strips, 3½"-wide, rust (border)

3 panels, 20" x 76", backing fabric (backing)

4 strips, 2½"-wide, backing fabric (seam covers)

7 strips, 2½"-wide, rust (binding)

## INSTRUCTIONS

**Blocks**

*Note: Work with the same leaf fabric throughout each block.*

Diagram 1

1. Place 3⅜" blue background square right sides together with 3⅜" green leaf fabric. Draw diagonal line on wrong side of blue square. (**Diagram 1**)

2. Sew ¼" from each side of drawn line. (**Diagram 2**)

Diagram 2

3. Cut along drawn line to make two half-square triangles. (**Diagram 3**)

4. Repeat steps 1 to 3 for another pair of half-square triangles.

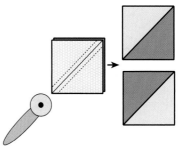

Diagram 3

5. For leaf stem, cut one 3" blue square in half diagonally to make two triangles. Sew 1" x 4¼" green strip to diagonal edges of each triangle. (**Diagram 4**) Trim corners. (**Diagram 5**)

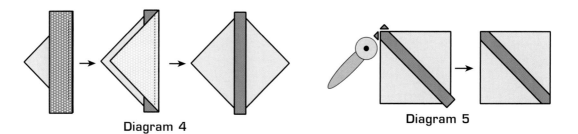

Diagram 4

Diagram 5

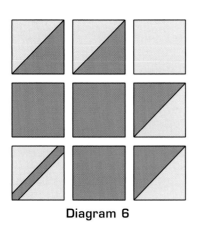

Diagram 6

6. Place four half-square triangles, one 3" background square, three 3" green squares, and stem square in three rows of three. (**Diagram 6**)

7. Sew together in rows, then sew rows together to complete Leaf block. (**Diagram 7**)

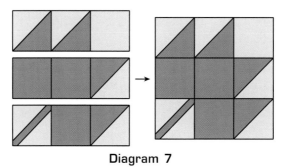

Diagram 7

8. Repeat steps 1 to 7 for six more green Leaf blocks, seven gold Leaf blocks, seven rust Leaf blocks and six brown Leaf blocks.

**Diagram 8**

## Finishing

1. Referring to photo or layout, place Leaf blocks alternately with fall print squares in nine rows of six.

2. Sew blocks together in pairs, then sew pairs into three panels. **(Diagram 8)**

3. Sew a 3¹/₂" x 15¹/₂" rust strip to top and bottom of each panel. **(Diagram 9)**

**Diagram 9**

4. For sashing, sew two 2¹/₂" rust strips together, then cut to 68"; repeat.

5. For side borders, sew two 3¹/₂" rust strips together, then cut to 68"; repeat.

# FREE FALL

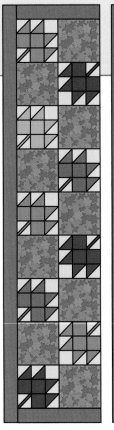
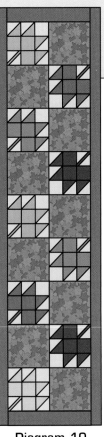
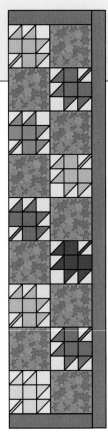

**Diagram 10**

6. Sew 2¹/2"-wide sashing strip to each side of middle panel. Sew a 3¹/2"-wide border strip to left side of first panel and other strip to right side of third panel. **(Diagram 10)**

**Free Fall Layout**

7. Layer panels with batting and backing. Quilt as desired.

8. Sew panels with right sides together. Hide seams referring to Covering the Seams, page 9.

9. Bind quilt referring to Adding Continuous Binding, page 10.

# ALTERNATE INSTRUCTIONS USING THE EASY ANGLE™ TOOL

**Blocks**

1. Cut the following:

   27 squares, 8" x 8", fall print
   10 strips, 3"-wide, blue background fabric
   4 strips each, 3"-wide, rust, brown, green, gold

2. Place a background strip right sides together with a green strip. With the Easy Angle™, cut four pairs of triangles, three green squares and two background squares. **(Diagram 1)** Keep pairs of triangles together.

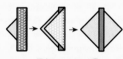
Diagram 1

3. Sew pairs of triangles together to make four half-square triangles. **(Diagram 2)**

Diagram 2

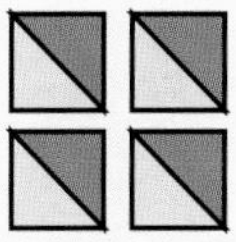

4. For stem, cut a 1" x 4$\frac{1}{4}$" strip from green fabric. Sew to diagonal edges of background triangles. **(Diagram 3)**

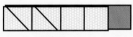
Diagram 3

5. Place four half-square triangles, one 3" background square, three 3" green squares and stem square in three rows of three. **(Diagram 4)**

Diagram 4

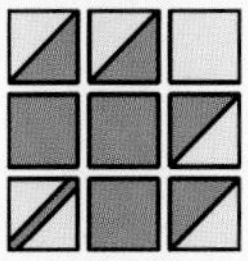

6. Sew together in rows, then sew rows together to complete Leaf block. **(Diagram 5)**

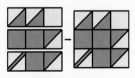
Diagram 5

7. Repeat steps 1 to 6 for six more green Leaf blocks, seven gold Leaf blocks, seven rust Leaf blocks and six brown Leaf blocks.

8. Refer to Finishing instructions on pages 43 and 44 to complete quilt.

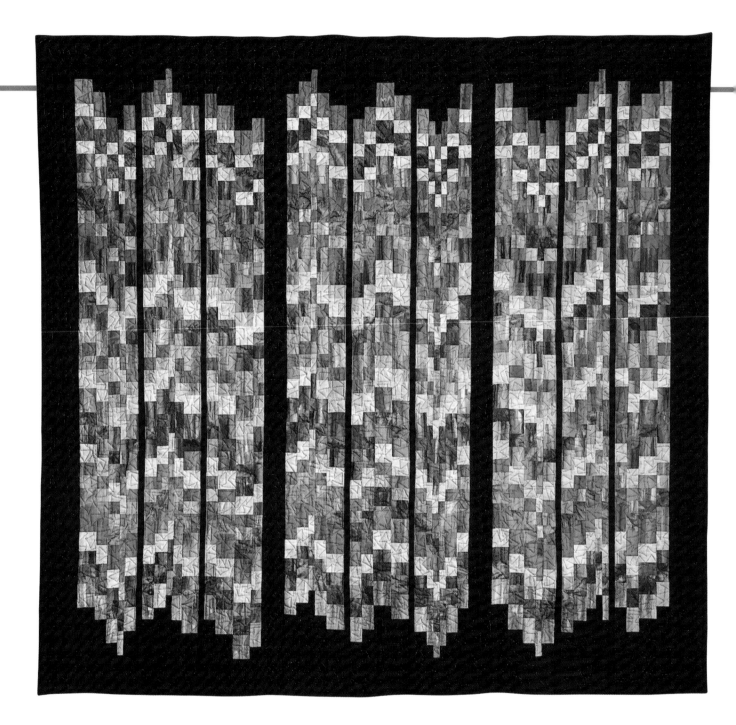

# BARGELLO DANCE

Approximate Size: 56 1/2" x 53 1/2"

## MATERIALS

1/2 yard of 5 different fabrics
(2 of the same fat quarters will work.)

3 yards black (borders, sashing, binding)

4 yards backing (backing, seam covers)

1 package Roll and Quilt™ batting

## CUTTING

### Panels

Cut each 1/2 yard piece into two 22" x 18" pieces.
Layer these pieces on top of each other. Then
cut the following from each set:

  3 strips, 1 1/2" x 22"

  3 strips, 2" x 22"

  3 strips, 2 1/2" x 22"

### Finishing

3 strips, 9"-wide, black (top and bottom
border)
cut into 22" x 9" strips

4 strips, 4" x 44", black (side borders)

4 strips, 2 1/2" x 44", black (sashing)

12 strips, (1" x 44"), black (inside spacers)

6 strips, 2 1/2"-wide, black (binding)

4 strips, 2 1/2"-wide, backing fabric (seam covers)

3 panels, 20" x 55", backing fabric (backing)

47

## INSTRUCTIONS

1. On a flat surface, set strips in a pleasing order. Be sure to make three panels exactly the same. **(Diagram 1)**

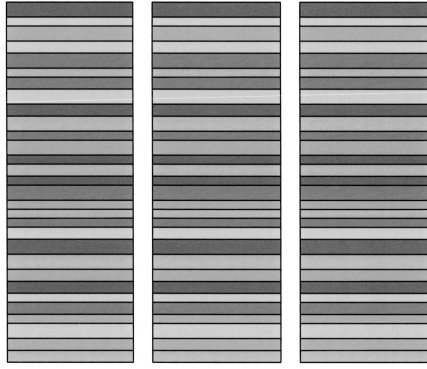

**Diagram 1**

2. Sew strips together being careful not to stretch the strips as you are sewing. Continue sewing until you have about 12" of strips, then sew another set. Continue sewing until all strips are sewn. **Note:** *Sewing only 12" or so of strips will prevent over handling of the fabric.* **(Diagram 2)**

**Hint:** *Place a piece of masking tape in the upper left corner of each set. By doing this, you will always know which side is up.* **(Diagram 3)**

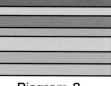

Diagram 2

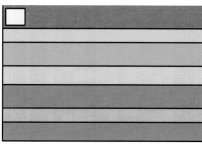

Diagram 3

3. Press seams open.

4. Sew all the sets together to complete a panel. Repeat with other sets to have three identical panels. **(Diagram 4)**

5. Trim all the panels so they are the same width. (about 21¹/₂" or 22")

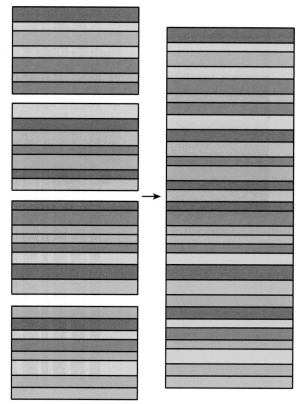

Diagram 4

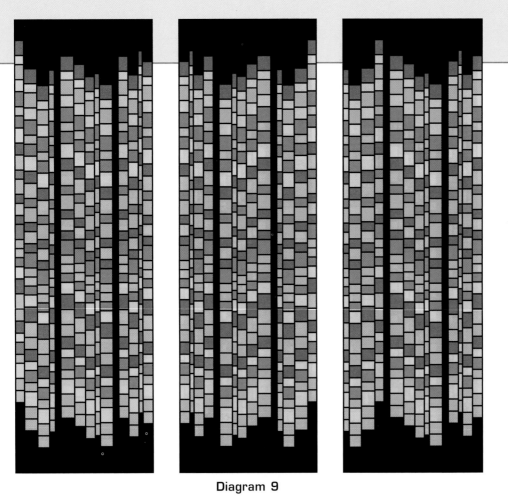

Diagram 9

11. Repeat for two more panels.

12. Trim the uneven top and bottom edges of each panel so that each panel is the same length. **(Diagram 9)**

13. Measure length of panels and cut two 2¹/₂"-wide black strips and two 4"-wide black strips to that length. Sew a 2¹/₂" black strip to each side of center panel. Sew a 4" black strip to left side of first panel and another 4" black strip to right side of last panel. **(Diagram 10)**

14. Layer panels with backing and batting. Quilt as desired.

15. Sew panels with right sides together. Hide seams referring to Covering the Seams, page 9.

16. Bind quilt referring to Adding Continuous Binding, page 10.

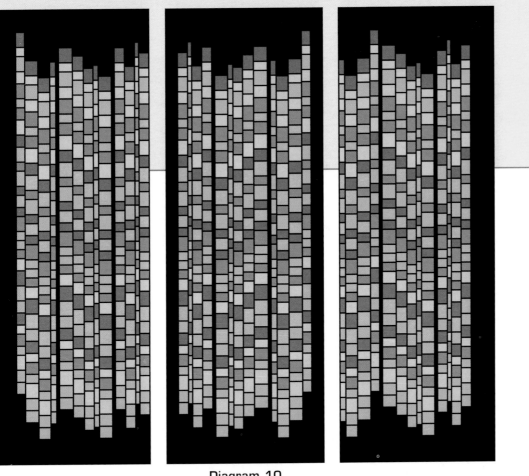

Diagram 10

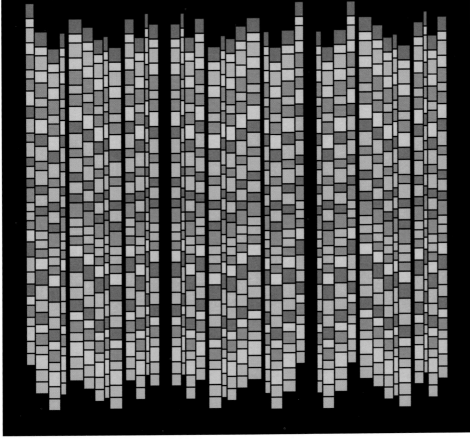

Bargello Dance Layout

53

54

# STAR SHINE

Approximate Size: 53" x 68"

## MATERIALS

3 yards dark brown (Large Stars, second border, binding)

2 1/2 yards medium brown (background, cornerstones)

1 yard gold (Small Stars, first border)

4 3/4 yards backing fabric (includes seam covers)

1 package Roll and Quilt™ batting

## CUTTING

### Blocks

96 squares, 3 1/2" x 3 1/2", dark brown

12 squares, 6 1/2" x 6 1/2", dark brown

17 rectangles, 6 1/2" x 9 1/2", medium brown

14 rectangles, 3 1/2" x 6 1/2", medium brown

10 rectangles, 3 1/2" x 9 1/2", medium brown

28 squares, 3 1/2" x 3 1/2", medium brown (Small Stars and finishing)

12 squares, 3 7/8" x 3 7/8", medium brown (Small Star)

12 squares, 3 7/8" x 3 7/8", gold (Small Star)

6 squares, 3 1/2" x 3 1/2", gold (Small Star)

*cutting directions continue on page 56*

Diagram 13

2. Sew 2" x 9 1/2" gold strips to 4 1/2" x 9 1/2" dark brown strips, then sew to top and bottom of first panel. Sew 2" x 15 1/2" gold strips to 4 1/2" x 15 1/2" dark brown strips, then sew to top and bottom of second and third panels. Sew 2" x 3 1/2" gold strips to 4 1/2" x 3 1/2" dark brown strips then sew to top and bottom of fourth panel. **(Diagram 13)**

3. Sew two 2"-wide gold strips together, then cut strip 57 1/2" long. Repeat.

4. Sew two 4 1/2"-wide dark brown strips together, then cut strip 57 1/2" long. Repeat.

5. Sew a 2" x 57 1/2" gold strip to dark brown strip. Repeat.

6. Sew a 6" medium brown square to each end of each border strip. Sew one border strip to left side of first panel and other border strip to right side of fourth panel. **(Diagram 14)**

**Diagram 14**

7. Layer each panel with batting and backing. Quilt as desired.

8. Sew panels together with right sides together. Hide seams referring to Covering the Seams, page 9.

9. Bind quilt referring to Adding Continuous Binding, page 10.

**Star Shine Layout**

## ALTERNATE INSTRUCTIONS USING EASY ANGLE™ AND COMPANION ANGLE™ TOOLS

1. For Small Stars, cut two 3¹/₂" strips from gold print and four 3¹/₂" strips from medium brown, then cut six squares from gold print and 24 squares from medium brown.

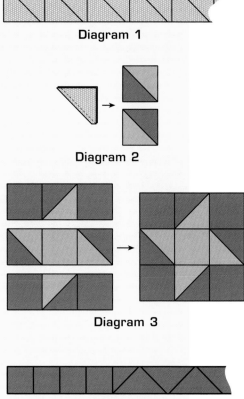

Diagram 1

2. Place remaining gold and medium brown strips right sides together. Cut 24 triangle sets using the Easy Angle™ tool. (**Diagram 1**)

3. Sew the triangle pairs together to form half-square triangles. Press seam toward gold fabric. (**Diagram 2**)

Diagram 2

4. Place half-square triangles and squares in three rows of three. Sew together in rows, then sew rows together to complete Small Star. (**Diagram 3**)

5. For Connecting blocks, cut 17 rectangles, 6¹/₂" x 9¹/₂" from medium brown print and 68 squares, 3¹/₂" x 3¹/₂", from dark brown print. Follow steps 5 to 8 on pages 57 and 58.

Diagram 3

6. To finish Large Star points, cut two 3¹/₂" strips from medium brown. First cut four 3¹/₂" squares, then cut 14 triangles using the Companion Angle™ tool. (**Diagram 4**)

Diagram 4

7. Cut two 3¹/₂"-wide strips from dark brown, then cut 28 triangles using the Easy Angle™ tool.

8. Sew a dark brown triangle to each diagonal edge of medium brown triangle. Repeat 13 more times. (**Diagram 5**)

Diagram 5

9. Follow steps 1 to 9, pages 59 to 61 to complete quilt.

# NATURE STUDIES NINE PATCH

Approximate Size: 46" x 64"

## MATERIALS

5 fat quarters assorted light prints

5 fat quarters assorted dark prints

$1/3$ yard accent color

1 yard dark print (border, binding)

4 yards backing (includes seam covers)

1 package Roll and Quilt™ batting

## CUTTING

**Blocks**

From each light and dark print fat quarter cut:

5 squares, $3^1/2$" x $3^1/2$"

18 squares, $3^7/8$" x $3^7/8$"

**Finishing**

4 strips, $1^1/2$" x $9^1/2$", accent fabric (first border)

2 strips, $1^1/2$" x $18^1/2$", accent fabric (first border)

4 strips, $1^1/2$"-wide, accent fabric (first border)

4 strips, $4^1/2$" x $10^1/2$", dark print (second border)

2 strips, $4^1/2$" x $18^1/2$", dark print (second border)

4 strips, $4^1/2$"-wide, dark print (second border)

7 strips, $2^1/2$"-wide, dark print (binding)

4 strips, $2^1/2$"-wide, backing fabric (seam covers)

3 panels, 20" x 66", backing fabric (backing)

64

## INSTRUCTIONS

### Blocks

*Note:* Work with the same light and dark fabrics throughout each block.

1. For Nine-Patch block, place a 3⁷/₈" light square right sides together with a 3⁷/₈" dark square. Draw a diagonal line on wrong side of light square. **(Diagram 1)**

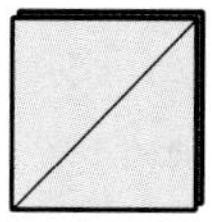

**Diagram 1**

2. Sew ¹/₄" from each side of drawn line. **(Diagram 2)**

**Diagram 2**

3. Cut along drawn line to make two half-square triangles. **(Diagram 3)**

4. Repeat with four more pairs of squares. You will use seven half-square triangles for each block.

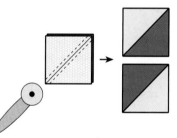

**Diagram 3**

5. Place half-square triangles and one 3¹/₂" light print square and one 3¹/₂" dark print square according to **Diagram 4**.

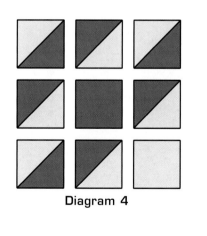

**Diagram 4**

6. Sew together in rows, then sew rows together to complete Nine Patch block. **(Diagram 5)**

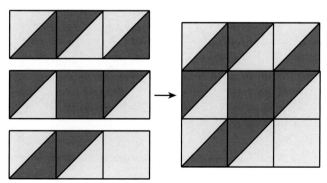

**Diagram 5**

7. Repeat steps 1 to 6 to make 23 more Nine Patch blocks. Use different combinations for a more scrappy look.

**Finishing**

1. Arrange blocks in a pleasing arrangement of six rows with four blocks in each.

2. Sew blocks together in three panels. **(Diagram 6)**

**Diagram 6**

3. Sew 1$\frac{1}{2}$" x 9$\frac{1}{2}$" accent fabric strips to top and bottom of first and third panels. Sew 1$\frac{1}{2}$" x 18$\frac{1}{2}$" accent fabric strips to top and bottom of second panel. **(Diagram 7)**

Diagram 7

Diagram 8

4. Piece two 1¹/₂"-wide accent fabric strips; cut to 56¹/₂" long. Repeat. Sew one strip to left side of first panel and other strip to right side of third panel. **(Diagram 8)**

5. Sew 4¹/₂" x 10¹/₂" dark print strips to top and bottom of first and third panels. Sew 4¹/₂" x 18¹/₂" dark print strips to top and bottom of second panel. Piece two 4¹/₂"-wide dark print strips; cut to 64¹/₂" long. Repeat. Sew one strip to left side of first panel and other strip to right side of third panel. **(Diagram 9)**

6. Layer each panel with batting and backing. Quilt as desired.

7. Sew panels together with right sides together. Hide seams referring to Covering the Seams, page 9.

8. Bind quilt referring to Adding Continuous Binding, page 10.

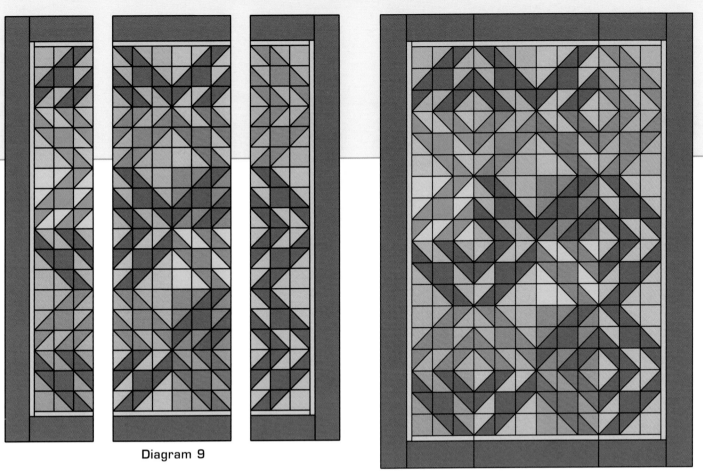

Diagram 9

Nature Studies Nine Patch Layout

## ALTERNATE INSTRUCTIONS USING THE EASY ANGLE™ TOOL

1. Cut each light and dark fat quarter into 3½" strips.

2. Place one dark strip and one light strip with right sides together. Cut one 3½" square and seven triangles using the Easy Angle™ tool. **(Diagram 1)**

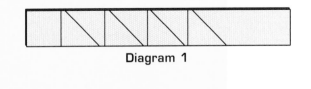

Diagram 1

3. Sew the light and dark triangles together to make half-square triangles. **(Diagram 2)** Press toward dark fabric.

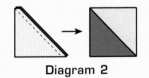

Diagram 2

4. Follow steps 5 to16, pages 65 to 68, to complete quilt.

# HERE'S MY HEART

Approximate Size: 56" x 56"

## MATERIALS

- 1¼ yards dark pink (hearts, binding)
- 1¼ yards light pink (background)
- 2 yards medium pink (background, border)
- 4 yards backing fabric (includes seam covers)
- 1 package Roll and Quilt™ batting

## CUTTING

**Blocks**

- 26 squares, 4½" x 4½", dark pink (Hearts)
- 13 squares, 4⅞" x 4⅞", dark pink (Hearts)
- 9 squares, 4⅞" x 4⅞", medium pink (Hearts)
- 4 squares, 4⅞" x 4⅞", light pink (Hearts)
- 36 squares, 1¾" x 1¾", medium pink (Hearts)
- 16 squares, 1¾" x 1¾", light pink (Hearts)
- 9 squares, 9¼" x 9¼", medium pink cut in quarters diagonally
- 6 squares, 9¼" x 9¼", light pink cut in quarters diagonally
- 4 squares, 4½" x 4½", light pink
- 8 rectangles, 4½" x 8½", light pink
- 12 squares, 4⅞" x 4⅞", light pink cut in half diagonally

71

*cutting directions continue on page 72*

**Finishing**

   2 strips, 4$^{1}/_{2}$" x 12$^{1}/_{2}$", medium pink (border)

   2 strips, 4$^{1}/_{2}$" x 16$^{1}/_{2}$", medium pink (border)

   2 strips, 4$^{1}/_{2}$" x 20$^{1}/_{2}$", medium pink (border)

   4 strips, 4$^{1}/_{2}$"-wide, medium pink (border)

   4 strips, backing fabric (seam covers)

   2 panels, 20" x 60", backing fabric (backing)

   1 panel, 28" x 60", backing fabric (backing)

   7 strips, 2$^{1}/_{2}$"-wide, dark pink (binding)

## INSTRUCTIONS

### Blocks

Diagram 1

1. For hearts, place a 1$^{3}/_{4}$" medium pink square right sides together at upper right corner of a 4$^{1}/_{2}$" dark pink square. **(Diagram 1)**

2. Sew diagonally across small square. Trim $^{1}/_{4}$" from seam allowance and flip resulting triangle over. **(Diagram 2)** Press.

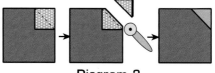

Diagram 2

3. Repeat at upper left corner of dark pink square. **(Diagram 3)**

Diagram 3

**Diagram 4**

4. Repeat for another square. Sew both squares together for top of heart. **(Diagram 4)**

5. Place a 4⅞" dark pink square right sides together with a 4⅞" medium pink square. Draw a diagonal line from corner to corner on wrong side of medium pink square. **(Diagram 5)**

**Diagram 5**

6. Sew ¼" from each side of drawn line. **(Diagram 6)**

**Diagram 6**

7. Cut along drawn line to make two half-square triangles; sew together for bottom of heart. **(Diagram 7)**

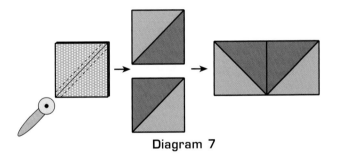

**Diagram 7**

8. Sew top and bottom heart sections together to complete Heart block. **(Diagram 8)**

9. Repeat steps 1 to 8 for eight more Heart blocks with medium pink background and four with light pink background.
**(Diagram 9)**

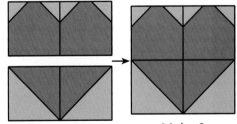

Make 9
**Diagram 8**

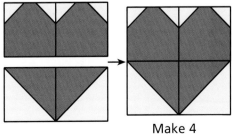

Make 4
**Diagram 9**

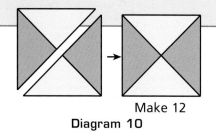

**Make 12**
**Diagram 10**

10. For alternate blocks, sew a light pink triangle to medium pink triangle; repeat. Sew together to complete block. (**Diagram 10**) Repeat for 11 more blocks.

11. For finishing rectangles, sew small light pink triangles to large medium pink triangles. (**Diagram 11**) Repeat for 11 more rectangles.

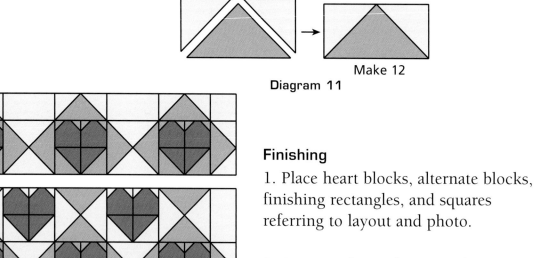

**Make 12**
**Diagram 11**

### Finishing

1. Place heart blocks, alternate blocks, finishing rectangles, and squares referring to layout and photo.

2. Sew together in horizontal panels. (**Diagram 12**)

**Diagram 12**

3. Sew 4¹/₂" x 12¹/₂" border strips to sides of top panel, 4¹/₂" x 16¹/₂" border strips to sides of middle panel and 4¹/₂" x 20¹/₂" border strips to sides of bottom panel. **(Diagram 13)**

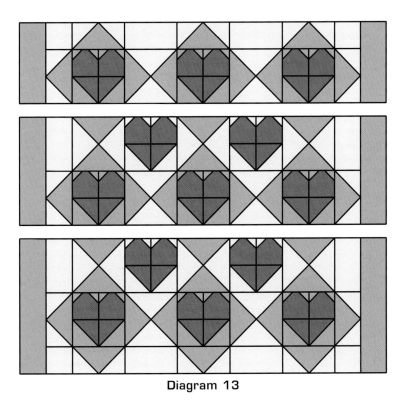

Diagram 13

4. Sew two 4¹/₂"-wide medium pink border strips together and cut to 56¹/₂" long; repeat.

5. Sew a border strip to upper edge of top panel and other strip to bottom edge of bottom panel. **(Diagram 14)**

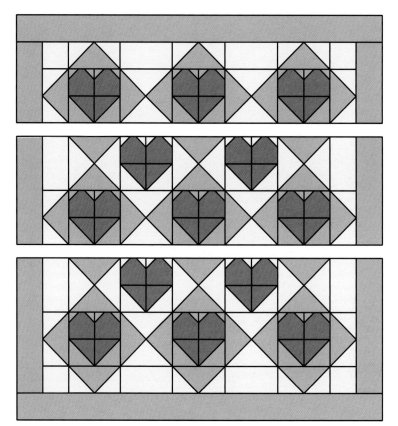

Diagram 14

6. Layer panels with batting and backing. Quilt as desired. *Note: The third panel is wider than the width of the batting strips. Therefore, place two 60" long strips next to each other and hand stitch large X's to join.* **(Diagram 15)**

76

Diagram 15

7. Sew quilted panels together with right sides together. Hide seams referring to Covering the Seams, page 9.

8. Bind quilt referring to Adding Continuous Binding, page 10.

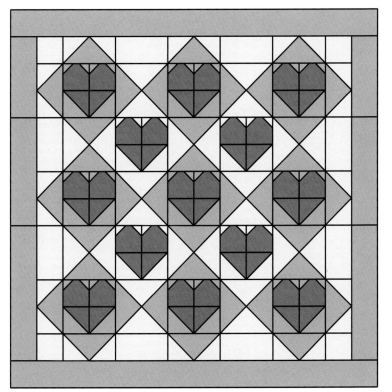

**Here's My Heart Layout**

## ALTERNATE INSTRUCTIONS USING EASY ANGLE™ AND COMPANION ANGLE™ TOOLS

### Cutting

5 strips, 4½"-wide, dark pink
cut 26 squares from 3 of these strips

13 strips, 4½"-wide, medium pink

2 strips, 1¾"-wide, medium pink
cut into 36 squares

1 strip, 1¾"-wide, light pink
cut into 16 squares

8 strips, 4½"-wide, light background
cut into 4 squares, 4½" x 4½"
    8 rectangles, 4½" x 8½"
    24 Easy Angle™ triangles
    24 Companion Angle™ triangles

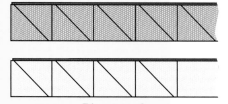

Diagram 1

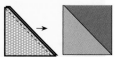

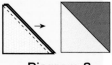

Diagram 2

### INSTRUCTIONS

1. Place two dark pink strips right sides together with two medium pink strips. Cut 18 Easy Angle™ triangles. Place light pink strip right sides together with remaining dark pink strip. Cut eight Easy Angle™ triangles. **(Diagram 1)**

Diagram 3

2. Sew medium pink triangles to dark pink triangles for a total of 18 half-square triangles. Sew light pink triangles to dark pink triangles for a total of eight half-square triangles. **(Diagram 2)**

3. Cut five of the 4½" medium pink strips into triangles using the Companion Angle™ tool on the 8" finish line. **(Diagram 3)**

4. Follow Block instructions, pages 72 to 74, to complete blocks.

5. Follow Finishing instructions, pages 74 to 77, to complete quilt.

# WINTER PINES

Approximate Size: 60" x 70"

## MATERIALS

- 1/3 yard each, 3 different greens (trees)
- 1/3 yard each, 3 different backgrounds
- 1 yard dark blue print (squares on point)
- 3/4 yard light print (background for squares)
- 1 yard red print (sashing, first border)
- 1 1/4 yard dark blue print (second border, binding)
- 4 1/2 yards backing (includes seam covers)
- 1 package Roll and Quilt™ batting

## CUTTING

### Tree Blocks

From each of 3 different green prints, cut the following:

- 20 squares, 2 7/8" x 2 7/8"
- 8 rectangles, 2 1/2" x 4 1/2"
- 8 rectangles, 2 1/2" x 3 1/2"
- 8 rectangles, 2 1/2" x 1 1/2"
- 2 squares, 2 1/2" x 2 1/2"

*cutting directions continue on page 81*

79

80

From each of 3 different background prints, cut the following:

20 squares, $2^7/8$" x $2^7/8$"

8 rectangles, $2^1/2$" x $4^1/2$"

8 rectangles, $2^1/2$" x $3^1/2$"

8 rectangles, $2^1/2$" x $1^1/2$"

2 squares, $2^1/2$" x $2^1/2$"

**Squares on Point**

24 squares, $4^3/4$" x $4^3/4$", dark blue print

10 squares, $7^1/4$" x $7^1/4$", light background
cut diagonally into quarters

6 squares, $3^7/8$" x $3^7/8$", light background
cut diagonally in half

**Finishing**

12 strips, $2^1/2$"-wide, red print cut into:
6 strips, $2^1/2$" x $10^1/2$" (first vertical border)
6 strips, $2^1/2$" x $6^1/2$" (first vertical border)
7 strips, $2^1/2$" x $52^1/2$" (sashing, top/bottom border)

2 strips, 4" x $14^1/2$", dark blue print (side borders, row 1)

2 strips, 4" x $18^1/2$", dark blue print (side borders, row 2)

2 strips, 4" x $20^1/2$", dark blue print (side borders, row 3)

2 strips, 4" x $10^1/2$", dark blue print (side borders, row 4)

4 strips, 4"-wide, dark blue print (horizontal border)

8 strips, $2^1/2$"-wide, dark blue print (binding)

6 strips, $2^1/2$-wide, backing fabric (seam covers)

4 panels, 22" x 62", backing fabric (backing)

## INSTRUCTIONS

Diagram 1

### Tree Blocks

1. For Tree block, place a 2⁷/₈" green square right sides together with a 2⁷/₈" background square. Draw a diagonal line on wrong side of background square. (**Diagram 1**)

Diagram 2

2. Sew ¹/₄" from each side of drawn line. (**Diagram 2**)

3. Cut along drawn line for two half-square triangles. (**Diagram 3**)

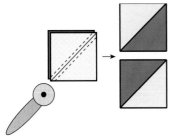

Diagram 3

4. Repeat steps 1-3 for remaining green and background squares for a total of 120 half-square triangles.

5. Place half-square triangles and remaining squares and rectangles in order referring to **Diagram 4**.

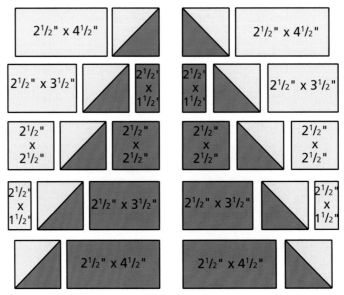

Diagram 4

6. Working with half of the block at a time, sew pieces in rows, then sew rows together.
**(Diagram 5)**

7. Sew halves together to complete a Tree block.
**(Diagram 6)**

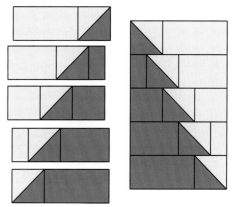

Diagram 5

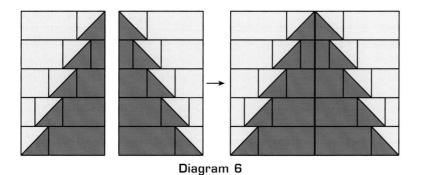

Diagram 6

8. Repeat steps 1 to 7 to complete 12 Tree Blocks.

**Finishing**

1. Sew four Tree blocks together. Make two more Tree rows.
**(Diagram 7)**

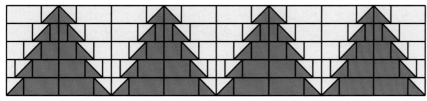

Diagram 7

2. For Squares on Point, sew eight 4³/4" dark blue print squares to 14 large and four small background triangles. **(Diagram 8)** Repeat for two more rows.

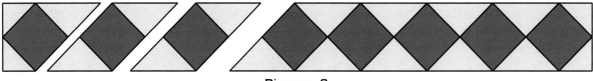

Diagram 8

3. Sew a 2¹/2" x 10¹/2" red print strip to each end of the Tree block rows. **(Diagram 9)**

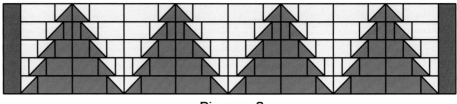

Diagram 9

4. Sew a 2¹/2" x 6¹/2" red print strip to each end of the Squares on Point rows. **(Diagram 10)**

Diagram 10

5. Referring to **Diagram 11**, sew 2¹/2" x 52¹/2" red print sashing strips to rows. You will have four horizontal panels. Do not sew them together yet.

**Diagram 11**

85

6. Sew 4" dark blue print border strips to each end of each row. **(Diagram 12)**

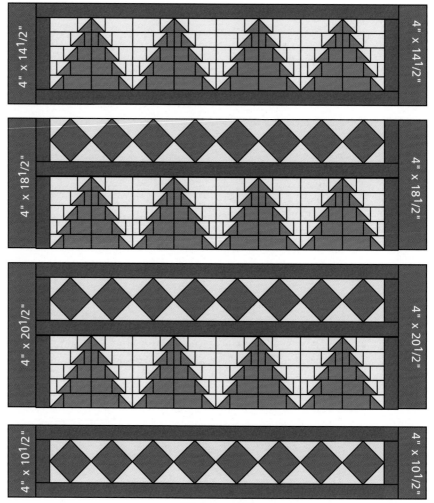

Diagram 12

7. Piece and cut 4" dark blue print strips to make two horizontal border strips, 59½" long. Sew a border strip to the top of first panel and the other border strip to the bottom of the fourth panel. **(Diagram 13)**

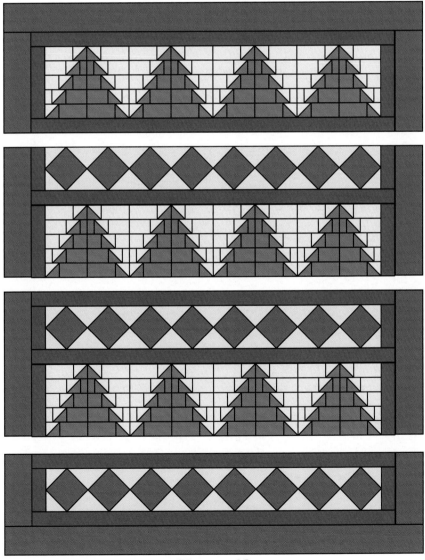

Diagram 13

8. Layer each panel with batting and backing. Quilt as desired.

9. Sew panels with right sides together. Hide seams referring to Covering the Seams, page 9.

10. Bind quilt referring to Adding Continuous Binding, page 10.

**Winter Pines Layout**

## ALTERNATE INSTRUCTIONS USING THE EASY ANGLE™ AND COMPANION ANGLE™ TOOLS

1. For the Tree blocks, cut 4 strips, 2½"-wide of each green print and 12 strips, 2½"-wide, of background fabric.

2. Fold each strip in half crosswise with right sides together.

3. Layer one folded green strip and one folded background strip. You will have 4 layers. (**Diagram 1**)

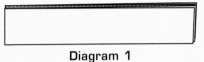

Diagram 1

4. Cut through all four layers using the Easy Angle™. (**Diagram 2**)

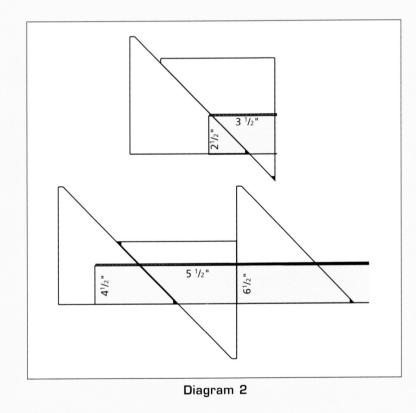

Diagram 2

92

2 squares, 15$\frac{1}{2}$" x 15$\frac{1}{2}$", light print (setting triangles)
cut diagonally in quarters

2 squares, 8" x 8", light print (corner triangles)
cut diagonally in half

**Finishing**

4 strips, 2$\frac{1}{2}$"-wide, medium print (sashing)

4 strips, 4" x 14$\frac{1}{2}$", medium print (top/bottom border)

2 strips, 4" x 18$\frac{1}{2}$", medium print (top/bottom border)

4 strips, 4"-wide, medium print (side borders)

3 panels, 20" x 68", backing (backing panels)

4 strips, 2$\frac{1}{2}$"-wide, backing (seam covers)

7 strips, 2$\frac{1}{2}$"-wide, medium print (binding)

## INSTRUCTIONS

### Basket Blocks

*Note: Work with one color throughout block.*

1. Place 3$\frac{3}{8}$" medium print square and 3$\frac{3}{8}$" floral print square right sides together. Draw diagonal line on wrong side of the lighter fabric. **(Diagram 1)**

Diagram 1

2. Sew $\frac{1}{4}$" from each side of drawn line. **(Diagram 2)**

Diagram 2

3. Cut along drawn line to make two half-square triangles. **(Diagram 3)**

4. Repeat steps 1 to 3 for another pair of squares.

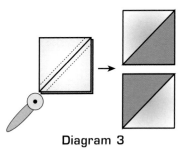

Diagram 3

93

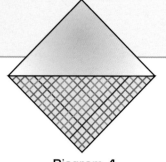

Diagram 4

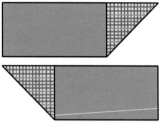

Diagram 5

5. Sew a large plaid triangle to a large floral triangle. **(Diagram 4)**

6. Sew a small plaid triangle to one end of 3" x 5½" rectangle; repeat, placing triangle on opposite side of rectangle. **(Diagram 5)**

7. Sew Basket block. **(Diagram 6)**

8. Repeat steps 1-7 for three more blocks for a single panel. Then repeat for remaining two panels. **(Diagram 7)**

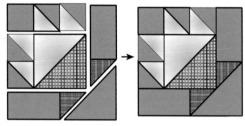

Diagram 6

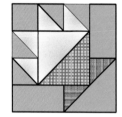

Diagram 7

**Finishing**

1. Sew blocks, setting triangles and corner triangles together to complete a panel. Repeat for two more panels. **(Diagram 8)**

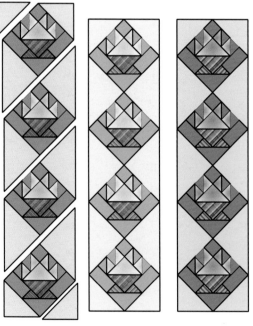

Diagram 8

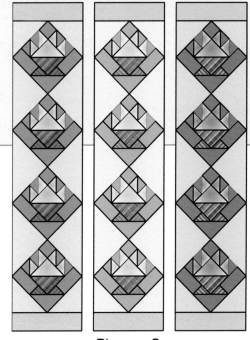

**Diagram 9**

2. Sew a 4"-wide border strip to top and bottom of each panel. **(Diagram 9)**

3. Sew a 2 1/2"-wide sashing strip to each side of second panel. Sew one 4"-wde strip to left side of first panel and other strip to right side of third panel. **(Diagram 10)**

4. Sew panels with right sides together. Hide seams referring to Covering the Seams, page 9.

5. Bind quilt referring to Adding Continuous Binding, page 10.

**Diagram 10**

**Happy Birthday Layout**

## ALTERNATE CUTTING INSTRUCTIONS USING THE EASY ANGLE™ TOOL

**For each 4-block panel, cut the following:**

1 strip, 5$^{1}/_{2}$", floral print
cut into 4 triangles using the Easy Angle™ tool **(Diagram 1)**

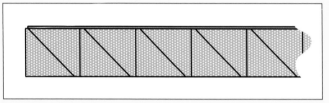

Diagram 1

2 strips, 3"-wide, floral print
cut into 16 triangles using the Easy Angle™ tool

1 strip, 5$^{1}/_{2}$", plaid
cut into 4 triangles using the Easy Angle™ tool

1 strip, 3"-wide, plaid
cut into 8 triangles using the Easy Angle™ tool

1 strip, 5$^{1}/_{2}$"-wide, medium print
cut into 4 triangles using the Easy Angle™ tool

3 strips, 3"-wide, medium print
cut into:
    8 rectangles, 3" x 5$^{1}/_{2}$"
    4 squares, 3" x 3"
    16 triangles using the Easy Angle™ tool

### Instructions

Follow instructions on pages 93 to 95 to make quilt.

# ALL STAR SALUTE

Approximate Size: 56½" x 68"

## MATERIALS

⅛ yard of 12 assorted dark fabrics (stars) or 1½ yards of the same fabric

Fat quarter of 12 assorted light fabrics (background) or 1½ yards of the same fabric

2 yards plaid (sashing, border)

1 yard red (binding, seam covers)

4 yards backing

1 package Roll and Quilt™ batting

Template plastic

## TEMPLATE (page 102)

Diamond

## CUTTING

### Blocks

1 strip, 3⅜"-wide, each dark fabric cut into 8 Diamonds

4 squares, 4⅞" x 4⅞", each light fabric cut in half diagonally

4 squares, 3⅜" x 3⅜", each light fabric cut in half diagonally

*cutting directions continue on page 99*

**Diagram 1**

**Finishing**

6 crosswise strips, 4½" x 13½", plaid (border)

9 crosswise strips, 2½" x 13½", plaid (sashing)

2 lengthwise strips, 4½" x 72", plaid (border)

4 lengthwise strips, 2½" x 72", plaid  (sashing)

7 strips, 2½"-wide, red (binding)

4 strips, 2½"-wide, red (seam covers)

3 panels, 20" x 72", backing (backing panels)

**Diagram 2**

# INSTRUCTIONS

## Blocks

1. Working with one block at a time, arrange Diamonds and Triangles into a star. (**Diagram 1**)

2. Sew a small Triangle to a Diamond. (**Diagram 2**) Press seam toward Diamond.

3. Sew a large Triangle to adjacent side of Diamond. (**Diagram 3**) Press seams toward Diamond. Repeat.

**Diagram 3**

4. Repeat for remaining Diamonds and Triangles. (**Diagram 4**)

5. Sew pieced triangles together to form quarters of the block. (**Diagram 5**)

**Diagram 4**

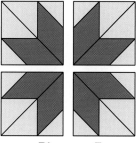

**Diagram 5**

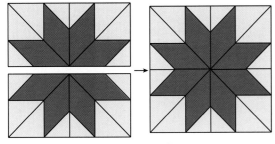

**Diagram 6**

6. Sew quarters to complete Star block.
**(Diagram 6)**

7. Repeat steps 1 to 6 for remaining blocks.

**Finishing**

1. Arrange Star blocks in a pleasing color arrangement.

2. Sew blocks together in vertical rows with 2½" x 13½" strips in between. Sew the 4½" x 13½" plaid strips to each end.
**(Diagram 7)**

**Diagram 7**

3. Sew 2$^{1}/_{2}$"-wide strips to each side of middle panel, to right side of first panel and left side of third panel. Sew 4$^{1}/_{2}$"-wide strips to left side of first panel and right side of third panel. **(Diagram 8)**

4. Layer panels with backing and batting. Quilt as desired.

5. Sew panels together with **backing** sides together. Hide seams referring to Covering the Seams, page 9. Note that seam covers become sashing on the front of the quilt.

6. Bind quilt referring to Adding Continuous Binding, page 10.

Diagram 8

**All Star Salute Layout**

## ALTERNATE CUTTING INSTRUCTIONS USING THE EASY EIGHT™ AND EASY ANGLE™ TOOLS

For each Block, cut the following:

1. For the Stars, cut a dark fabric strip on the 4" finished line of the Easy Eight™ tool. Cut eight Diamonds by sliding the tool across the strip. (**Diagram 1**)

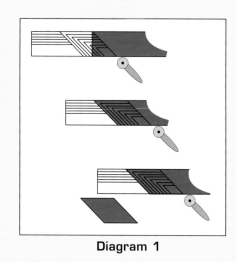

Diagram 1

2. For the background, cut a 4¹/₂"-wde strip from light fabric. Fold the strip in half. Cut four pairs of Easy Angle™ triangles from this strip. (**Diagram 2**)

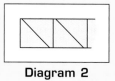

Diagram 2

3. Cut the remaining part of the strip, 4" wide and cut four pairs of Easy Angle™ triangles.

To finish quilt, follow instructions beginning on page 99.

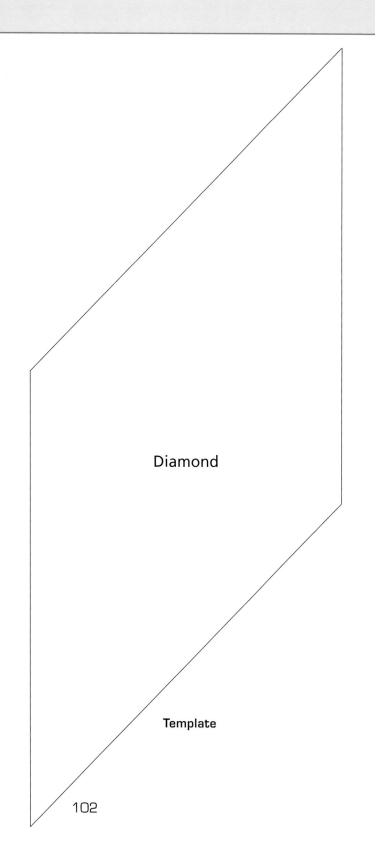

Diamond

Template

102

# STARS BY DESIGN

Approximate Size: 66½" x 74"

## MATERIALS

37 assorted fat eighths or 3 yards assorted fabrics (hexagons)

3 yards black (background, border, binding)

5¼ yards backing fabric

1 package Roll and Quilt™ batting

Template plastic

## TEMPLATES (page 109)

Hexagon

Trapezoid

Triangle

## CUTTING

### Blocks

22 Trapezoids, assorted fabrics
*Hint: Cut 3¹/8"-wide strips first.*

99 Hexagons, assorted fabrics
*Hint: Cut 5 3/4"-wide strips first.*

210 Triangles
*Hint: Cut 12 strips, 3¹/8"-wide, black first.*

*cutting directions continue on page 105*

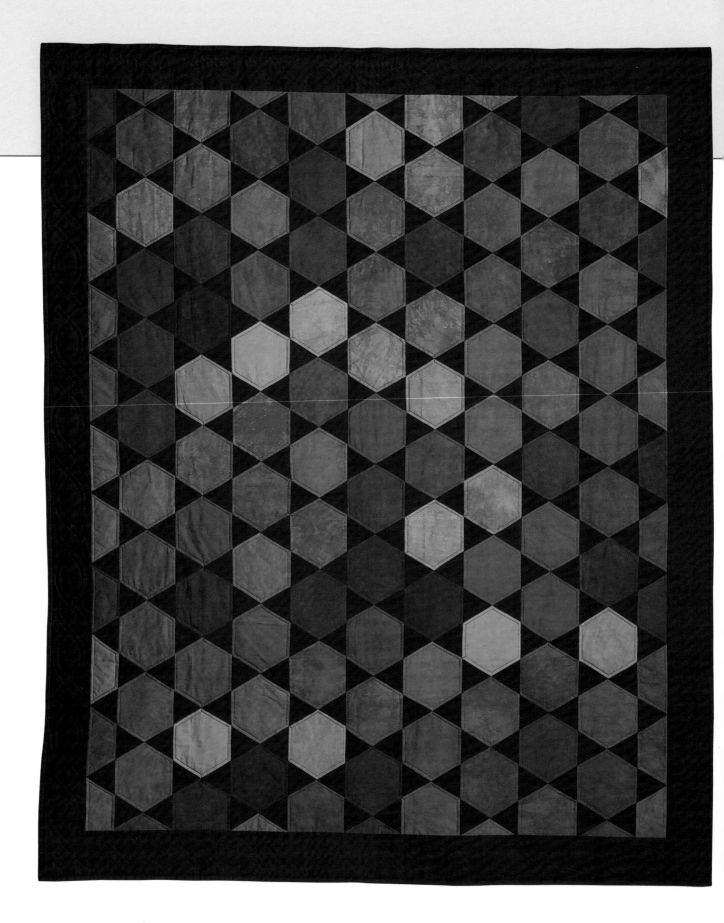

104

**Finishing**

   8 strips, 4 1/2"-wide, black (border)

   8 strips, 2 1/2"-wide, black (binding)

   6 strips, 2 1/2"-wide, backing (seam covers)

   4 panels, 20" x 78", backing (backing panels)

**Diagram 1**

## INSTRUCTIONS

### Units

1. Sew a triangle to upper right edge of a Hexagon. **Hint:** *Note which sides of the Hexagons are on the straight of grain. You can ravel a thread to see if it follows the cut edge. Keeping the straight of grain going up and down will make your quilt stronger.* **(Diagram 1)**

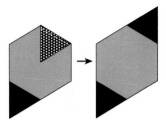

**Diagram 2**

2. Sew a Triangle to the opposite edge of the Hexagon. **(Diagram 2)**

**Diagram 3**

3. Continue until you have 91 Hexagon units. Cut five units in half. **(Diagram 3)**

4. Sew a Triangle to the upper right edge of four Hexagons and to the lower left edge of four more Hexagons. **(Diagram 4)**

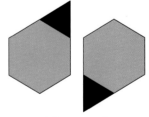

**Diagram 4**

5. Sew a Triangle to the left edge of a Trapezoid; repeat 19 more times. **(Diagram 5)** There will be two Trapezoids left over.

**Diagram 5**

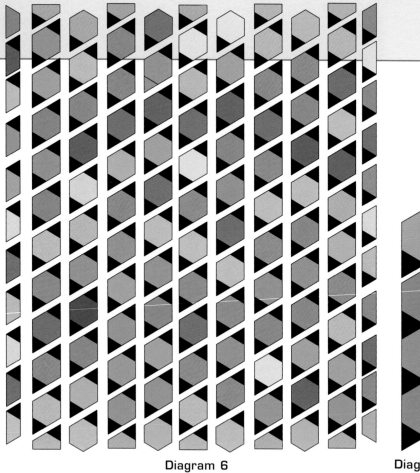

Diagram 6

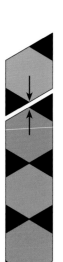

Diagram 7

**Finishing**

1. Referring to **Diagram 6**, place hexagon units, half units, and trapezoid units in vertical rows in a pleasing color arrangement.

2. Sew units together in vertical rows matching centers. **(Diagram 7)**

3. Sew rows together in panels. **(Diagram 8)**

Diagram 8

Diagram 9

4. Trim bottom and top edges of panels ¼" from tips of triangles. **(Diagram 9)**

5. Measure width of each panel and cut two 4½"-wide black strips for each panel to those measurements. Sew to top and bottom of each panel. **(Diagram 10)**

Diagram 10

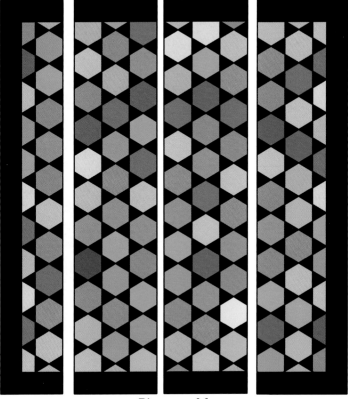

Diagram 11

6. Measure length of panels and cut two 4½"-wide black strips to that measurement. Sew one strip to the left side of the first panel and the other strip to the right side of the last panel. **(Diagram 11)**

107

## Finishing

6 strips, 6½" x 12½", medium gold (border)

8 strips, 6½"-wide, medium gold (sashing, border)

2 panels, 20" x 75", backing fabric (backing)

1 panel, 26" x 75", backing fabric (backing)

9 yards, 1¼"-wide bias strips, medium gold (binding)

## INSTRUCTIONS

### Blocks

1. Place light gold and green print 3⅞" squares right sides together. Draw a diagonal line on wrong side of light gold square. **(Diagram 1)**

Diagram 1

2. Sew ¼" from each side of drawn line. **(Diagram 2)**

Diagram 2

3. Cut along drawn line to make two half-square triangles. **(Diagram 3)**

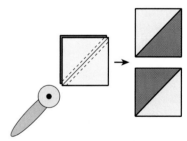

Diagram 3

4. Repeat steps 1 to 3 with remaining light gold and green print squares for a total of 60 half-square triangles.

5. Sew 3½" blue print square to half-square triangle. **(Diagram 4)** Repeat for all blue print squares and half-square triangles.

Diagram 4

6. Place petal pattern on top of pink floral rectangle. Trace, then cut curved edges. **(Diagram 5)**

Diagram 5

7. Turn curved edges under, ¼"; press. Position curved petal onto background rectangle. **(Diagram 6)**

Diagram 6

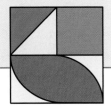

Diagram 7

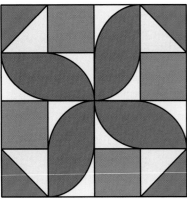

Diagram 8

8. Hand or machine stitch folded edge of petal pieces onto the background rectangle. **Hint:** *Use a very small blind hemstitch on your sewing machine with thread that matches the background fabric.*

9. Sew a petal to a unit made in step 5. Repeat 3 more times. **(Diagram 7)**

10. Sew four units from step 9 together to complete Windflower block. **(Diagram 8)** Repeat for 14 more blocks.

### Finishing

1. Sew five blocks together in a vertical row. **(Diagram 9)** Repeat 2 more times.

2. Sew a 6¹/₂" x 12¹/₂" border strip to top and bottom of each row. **(Diagram 10)**

3. Sew two 6¹/₂"-wide strips together, then cut so it is 72¹/₂" long. Repeat for three more strips.

Diagram 9

Diagram 10

Diagram 11

4. Sew sashing and border strips to rows to complete three panels. (**Diagram 11**)

5. Layer the panels with batting and backing. Quilt as desired. Note that the third panel is wider than 20" therefore, you will have to piece two pieces of batting together. Sew by hand with large "x's". (**Diagram 12**)

Diagram 12

6. Sew quilted panels with right sides together. Hide seams referring to Covering the Seams, page 9.

7. For scalloped edge, trace Scallop pattern (page 117) every 6" using a wash-away pencil. (**Diagram 13**)

8. Fold one raw edge of bias binding under ¼" along length. Place opposite raw edge next to drawn curved line. Stitch ¼" from edge of bias binding.

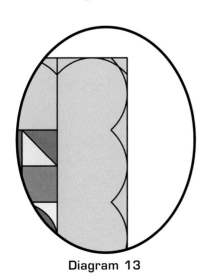

Diagram 13

9. After bias binding is attached, cut excess quilt away.

10. Turn binding over and hand stitch folded edge down.

**Windflower Layout**

## ALTERNATE INSTRUCTIONS USING EASY ANGLE™ TOOL

Follow Cutting and Instructions above except for the following:

1. Cut four strips, 3½"-wide from background fabric and four from green print. Then, cut 60 green print and 60 background triangles using the Easy Angle™ Tool. **(Diagram 1)**

2. Sew a green print and a background triangle together to make half-square triangle. **(Diagram 2)**

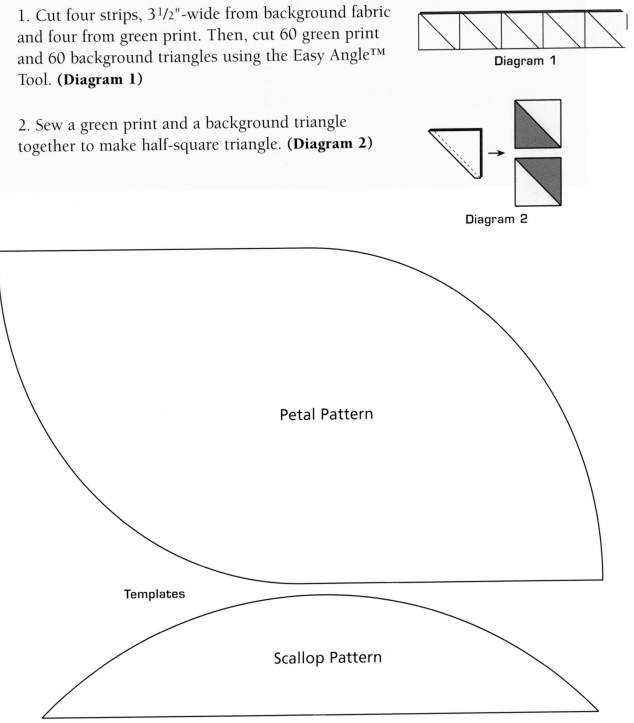

Diagram 1

Diagram 2

Petal Pattern

Templates

Scallop Pattern

118

# CUBES IN A ROW

Approximate Size: 45" x 58"

## MATERIALS

8 assorted fat quarters (cubes)

1 1/2 yards yellow (background)

1 yard green (second border, binding)

4 yards backing (includes seam covers)

1 package Roll and Quilt™ batting

Template plastic

## TEMPLATES (page 127)

Diamond

Triangle

## CUTTING

**Cubes**

5 strips each, 2 1/2"-wide, assorted fat quarters

6 strips, 4"-wide, yellow cut into 74 Triangles

*cutting directions continue on page 120*

**Finishing**

> 4 strips, 2¹/2" x 14¹/2", yellow (first horizontal border)
>
> 2 strips, 2¹/2" x 7¹/2", yellow (first horizontal border)
>
> 4 strips, 2¹/2"-wide, yellow (first vertical border)
>
> 2 strips, 3¹/2" x 16¹/2", green (second horizontal border)
>
> 2 strips, 3¹/2" x 14¹/2", green (second horizontal border)
>
> 2 strips, 3¹/2" x 9¹/2", green (second horizontal border)
>
> 4 strips, 3¹/2"-wide, green (second border)
>
> 7 strips, 2¹/2"-wide, green (binding)
>
> 4 strips, 2¹/2"-wide, backing fabric (seam covers)
>
> 3 panels, 20" x 62", backing fabric (backing)

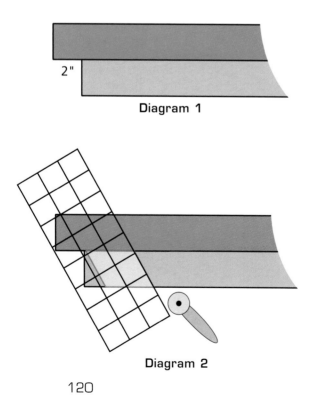

2"

**Diagram 1**

**Diagram 2**

## INSTRUCTIONS

### Blocks

1. Put all the assorted 2¹/2"-wide strips in a pile and mix them up. It is important to use the strips at random.

2. Sew strips together in pairs, placing the top strip 2" to the left of the bottom strip. **(Diagram 1)** Press seam.

3. Place Diamond template along edge of lower strip; carefully place acrylic ruler on top of template and cut to make a pair of Diamonds. **(Diagram 2)**

4. Continue cutting strips until you have 176 pairs of Diamonds.

5. Sew one pair of Diamonds to a matching pair of Diamonds. **(Diagram 3)** You will need 88 double Diamond sets.

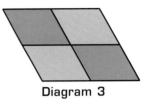

**Diagram 3**

6. Place three double Diamond sets together into a cube. **(Diagram 4)** You will need 28 cubes.

7. Sew two sets together starting ¹/₄" from top. **(Diagram 5)** Backstitch to lock stitches.

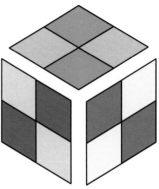

**Diagram 4**

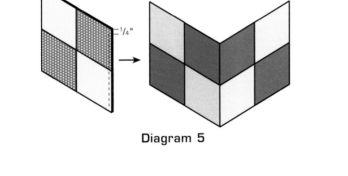

**Diagram 5**

8. Set in the top Diamond set, sewing from inside point to outside edge. **(Diagram 6)** Repeat for remaining cubes. You will have four double Diamond sets left over.

9. Sew a yellow Triangle to upper right and lower left edges of each cube. **(Diagram 7)**

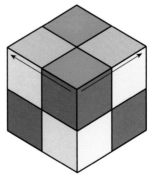

**Diagram 6**

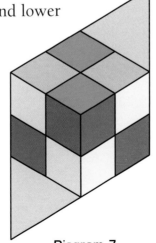

**Diagram 7**

121

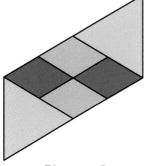

Diagram 8

10. Sew a yellow Triangle to upper right and lower left edges of the four double Diamond sets. **(Diagram 8)**

**Finishing**

1. Place cubes in five vertical rows. Rows 1, 3 and 5 have six blocks and rows 2 and 4 have five cubes with a double Diamond set at each end. Fill in with yellow Triangles. **(Diagram 9)**

Diagram 9

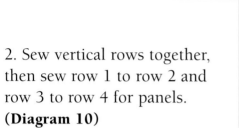

2. Sew vertical rows together, then sew row 1 to row 2 and row 3 to row 4 for panels. **(Diagram 10)**

3. Trim top and bottom edges of each panel ¹/₄" from Diamond. **(Diagram 11)**

Diagram 10

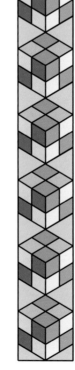

Diagram 11

4. Measure panels and cut two 2$\frac{1}{2}$"-wide yellow strips to each of those widths. Sew to top and bottom of each panel. **(Diagram 12)**

Diagram 12

5. Measure length of panels and cut two 2$\frac{1}{2}$"-wide yellow strips to that length. Sew one strip to left side of first panel and other strip to right side of last panel. (**Diagram 13**)

Diagram 13

# CUBES IN A ROW

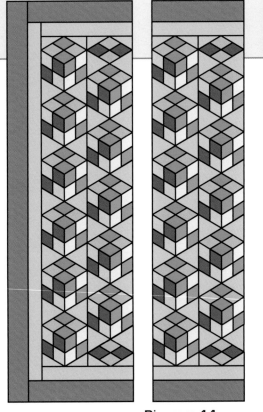

Diagram 14

6. Repeat steps 4 and 5 with $3\frac{1}{2}$"-wide green strips. **(Diagram 14)**

7. Layer each panel with backing and batting. Quilt as desired.

8. Sew panels with right sides together. Hide seams referring to Covering the Seams, page 9.

9. Bind quilt referring to Adding Continuous binding, page 10.

Cubes in a Row Layout

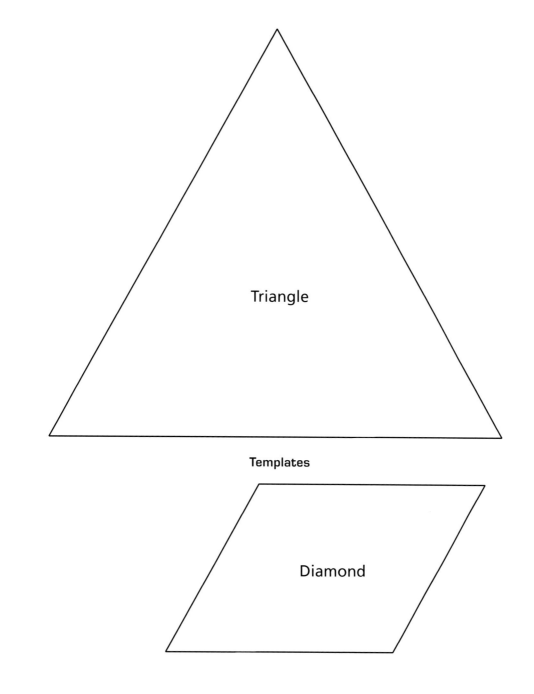

Triangle

**Templates**

Diamond

## ALTERNATE CUTTING INSTRUCTIONS USING THE EASY SIX™ AND EASY THREE™ TOOLS

1. Cut fat quarters with the Easy Six™ tool along the 2" finished edge. You will get 5 strips from each fabric.

2. Sew strips together in pairs, placing the top strip 2" to the left of the bottom strip. (**Diagram 1**) Press seam.

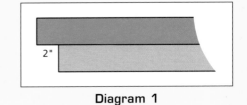

Diagram 1

3. Cut strips placing the Easy Six™ along the 2" finished line. (**Diagram 2**) You will need 176 strips.

4. Cut 6 strips from yellow placing the Easy Three™ tool along the 4" finished line. (**Diagram 3**) You will need 74 Triangles.

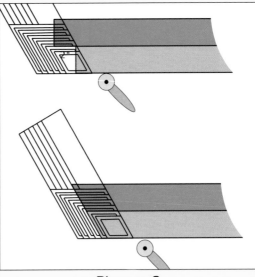

Diagram 2

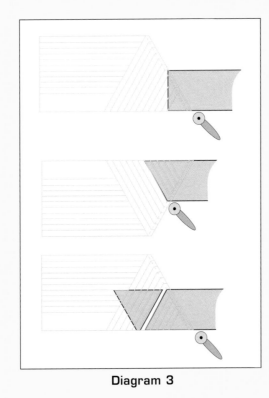

Diagram 3